Robert Goldston

was born in New York City and attended Columbia University. A former Guggenheim fellow, he has written novels, documentary film scripts, and many works of popular history. Mr. Goldston has traveled extensively and lived in England, France, and Spain. He now lives with his family in upstate New York.

Among Robert Goldston's highly acclaimed titles, many of which have been ALA Notable Books, are *The Russian Revolution, The Life and Death of Nazi Germany,* and *The Rise of Red China.* His most recent books include *The Road Between the Wars: 1918–1941,* which Booklist in a starred review called "A colorful, smoothly written, detailed treatment recommended as collateral reading for students or grist for history enthusiasts."

The Sword of the Prophet

A HISTORY OF THE ARAB WORLD

FROM THE TIME OF MOHAMMED

TO THE PRESENT DAY

Robert Goldston

FAWCETT CREST • **NEW YORK**

THE SWORD OF THE PROPHET

Published by Fawcett Crest Books, CBS Educational and Professional Publishing, a division of CBS Inc., by arrangement with The Dial Press.

ISBN: 0-449-24393-1

Maps by David Lindroth

Printed in the United States of America

First Fawcett Crest Printing: April 1981

12   11   10   9   8   7   6   5   4   3   2

For BILLY, MARTIN, and JOAQUIN KARAKAS

None but infidels gainsay the signs of God:
but let not their prosperity in
the land deceive thee.

Koran, XL

Contents

List of Maps

NOTE

Quotations from the Koran appearing in this book are from the translation made by J. M. Rodwell in 1861 as published in the Everyman's Library series by J. M. Dent (London, 1909). But while Rodwell rearranged the chronology of the chapters of the Koran to suit the scholarship of his day, the reader will find them here numbered according to the traditional Arabic system.

The calendar of Islam commences with the Prophet's migration (hejira) from Mecca to Medina in A.D. 622; furthermore it is a lunar calendar in which a year contains only some 355 days. Thus, for example, the date of publication of the most recent official Arabic text of the Koran in Cairo is A.D. 1925 according to the Christian calendar, but to the Moslem it is A.H. 1344 (year of the hejira). In this book, for ease of historical orientation, the prevalent Western system of dating has been used.

PROLOGUE

Three Weeks in October

On the morning of October 6, 1973, Americans awoke
to the excited voices of radio and television newscasters
announcing the sudden eruption of large-scale fighting
in the Near East. During the night (the eve of the
Jewish Yom Kippur holiday) specially trained commando units of the Egyptian army had ferried themselves across the Suez Canal and established bridge-
heads on its east bank. They were quickly followed by
massive Egyptian armored divisions which blasted
their way through the Israeli Bar-Lev defense line and
were now storming into the Sinai Desert beyond. In
apparent coordination with the Egyptian assault Syrian tank columns were reported to be advancing upon
Israel from the north. Israeli forces were everywhere
in retreat; casualties were heavy.

Americans were stunned. How had the Israelis,
those masters of the surprise maneuver, been themselves caught unaware? How had their fortified and

supposedly impregnable Bar-Lev line been so quickly pierced? Above all, why were they in retreat from *Arab* forces? Everyone knew that Arabs were not *real* fighters—that they lacked discipline, could not learn how to handle modern weapons, were badly disunited, and could hardly hope to master up-to-date military techniques.

But the Israeli retreat continued across the Sinai in the south and back up into the Golan Heights in the north. Israeli planes were having a difficult time establishing air control over the battlefields; Israeli tanks were being knocked out by the dozens and hundreds by new missile systems. On October 10 it was learned that the Soviet Union had started heavy shipments of arms and supplies to Egypt and Syria. For the first time since 1948 it appeared that Israel was in real danger of defeat. Everyone knew what that would mean. Once let those uncivilized Arab hordes loose in Jerusalem, Tel Aviv, Haifa, and a fearful massacre would take place, another holocaust.

Americans had done little to prevent the last holocaust—when Hitler's Nazi death factories had murdered more than six million Jews during World War II—and their consciences had never been easy since. This was an important factor in American support for Israel against every threat. The Jewish homeland was America's debt to the past, America's protégé, America's only ally in the entire Near East. American public opinion during the second week of October 1973 demanded action—speedy, large-scale action to save the young Jewish nation from extinction. Accordingly on October 13, President Richard M. Nixon announced that a massive American airlift had been organized and was even now delivering weapons to the embattled Israelis.

Thereafter the news from the Near East improved somewhat. The Israelis were able to hold off the Syrians in the north and even to push them back to within twenty-five miles of Damascus. With this front secured the Israelis turned all their forces back to the Sinai in the south. Across the arid wastes of that desert peninsula they dispatched a large tank force on a wide, daring sweep to outflank the Egyptian army. On October 15 this heavily armored column crossed the Suez Canal and then began driving north along its west bank toward the Egyptian canal city of Suez. Thus the Israelis threatened to completely cut off the Egyptian forces in Sinai from their home bases. It was a brilliant thrust that turned imminent defeat into stunning military victory. Americans breathed a sigh of relief.

But this time it appeared that the Arab nations were not fighting in isolation from each other. For on October 17 Americans heard that the Organization of Arab Petroleum-Exporting Countries (OPEC) had announced that its member nations, led by Saudi Arabia, were imposing a total embargo on shipments of oil to the United States and any other nation that supported the Israeli cause. Furthermore, oil production in those lands would be cut back 5 percent per month until the Israelis withdrew from occupied Arab territory. What did this mean? Could an oil embargo hurt the United States? While Americans puzzled over the matter, new and more ominous developments occurred.

On October 22, under pressure from the Soviet Union, both Egypt and Syria had accepted a United Nations call for a cease-fire, thereby preserving, as the Russians had hoped, at least some of their early gains. Israel, in agreement with the United States, had also agreed to the cease-fire. But this fragile truce had collapsed almost immediately, and Israeli forces had continued their advance toward the city of Suez. Unable to stem the Israeli tide, the Egyptians had asked that Russian and American troops under United Nations supervision be sent to the area as a peacekeeping force. When the Americans declined to intervene, the Russians threatened to send troops on their own. This would mean Soviet control of the entire region—something no American government could accept. It was while Soviet paratroopers were actually boarding their transports at airfields in the Ukraine that President Nixon ordered American forces throughout the world onto "Defense Condition Three." So in the early morning hours of October 25 the red war-alert lights began flashing on the control consoles of nuclear submarines running silently beneath the oceans and in missile silos deep within the Rocky Mountains. American commanders realized that similar lights must be flashing on similar consoles beneath the Russian Arctic ice cap and below the frozen tundra of Siberia. Armageddon—that last great battle of biblical prophecy which, fittingly enough, was to commence in the Near East—seemed about to explode. For several hours the world teetered on the brink of final catastrophe—and then the Russians backed down. They agreed to accept a UN peacekeeping force in the Near East from which both Russian and American troops would be excluded.

So the seventeen-day struggle that the Israelis would call the Yom Kippur War, and the Arabs the October War, came to its end. But during the following weeks and months, as the Arab oil embargo began taking effect and Americans found themselves lining up for hours on end at near-empty gas pumps while watching fuel prices (and hence all other prices) begin a dizzying upward spiral, they had both time and cause to reexamine some of their basic attitudes toward the Arab world.

Those attitudes were partly the result of simple ignorance; except in university postgraduate courses few Americans had ever bothered to study Arab history or civilization. But this ignorance itself was only a reflection of prejudice—it was due to a hangover of imperialistic arrogance from the era of Western domination of Islam.

Thus it had come as a surprise to learn that Arabs could fight and win battles—the descendants of those Arabs who had conquered half a world. It had come as a surprise that the Arab world could unite—that same

Arab world which had unitedly ruled a great empire for many centuries. Most shamefully of all, it had come as a surprise that Arabs could master the technology and scientific know-how of modern warfare—the heirs of those same Arabs from whom the West had learned so much of its basic science. The people of the United States could ill afford any more such unworthy surprises.

As Americans, under the pressure of urgent necessity, took a new look at the Arab world, the fog of prejudice began to lift from a colorful, noble, and fascinating historical landscape. In that landscape they could discern the real meaning of many hitherto puzzling movements and events—and in it too they could find the roots of much that was vital in their own past. For the history of Islam, it turned out, was an integral part of the heritage of all peoples, a part of the human story that had its origins in remote and even legendary times. . . .

CHAPTER ONE

The Year of the Elephant

In the Name of God, the Compassionate, the Merciful
Hast thou not seen how thy Lord dealt
with the army of the Elephant?
Did he not cause their stratagem to miscarry?

KORAN, CV

It was in A.D. 570, during the time of ignorance when men still worshiped idols and trees and stones and spirits, that the great Abraha, Christian king of Saba, marched upon the desert town of Mecca with a mighty host. His purpose, it was reported, was to utterly destroy this center of paganism and, in the name of Christ, put to the sword its heathen inhabitants. He was, it seemed, especially determined to raze the Kaaba of Mecca—the square stone temple in which abominations hateful to God were practiced. King Abraha's motives were, it appeared, irreproachably religious.

Nor did anyone, least of all the frightened citizens of Mecca, doubt the king's ability to carry out his threats. The Sabaean army was large, well trained, and equipped with spears, slings, bows, camels, and all the panoply of war; it even included a huge beast called an elephant to knock down walls and strike terror into enemy hearts. True, the Meccans, advised of Abraha's approach, might flee to the hills around their town, thereby escaping massacre; but if Mecca was destroyed, most of the fleeing refugees would starve to death in the arid desert anyhow. In their desperation the Meccans turned for advice and leadership to the oldest (he was seventy-five at the time) and wisest among them— Abdul Muttalib, a man of great holiness, the chief guardian of the Kaaba itself.

The fame of the Kaaba as a holy shrine extended far back into antiquity—perhaps to the very beginnings of time. For within the square temple was a great Black Stone, perhaps a meteorite, said to have been given to Adam when he was expelled from paradise. Since a blessing would surely fall upon any man who touched or kissed this rock, pilgrims from all over Arabia had made their way to Mecca since times immemorial. This was no doubt one of the reasons why Mecca had become a center of the desert trade routes extending north and south between the Indian Ocean and the Mediterranean Sea. So though it was unthinkable that the Meccans should charge or tax pilgrims for the privilege of worshiping in the Kaaba (on the contrary, they were honor bound to give food and precious water to their devout guests during the three days of religious ceremonies), they prospered from the commerce of the pilgrim caravans.

Abdul Muttalib was very much aware of the commercial as well as the religious importance of the Kaaba—for he was the great-great-grandson of Qusai, the clever chief of the Quraish tribe who more than a century earlier had seized Mecca with his Bedouin (from the Arabic *bedawi*, meaning "desert dwellers") kinsmen and reorganized the entire town. It was Qusai who caused the Meccans to build houses around the Kaaba; previously it had been the only building in a town of tents. It was Qusai who fixed the time of the annual pilgrimage to the Kaaba in the autumn of the year. It was Qusai who first organized the great trade fairs held during the month of pilgrimage in the valleys around Mecca; and, finally, it was Qusai who established the Council of Elders of the tribe of Quraish to rule the city. As the direct descendant of Qusai, Abdul Muttalib was chief of the council in his day.

We record all these facts as if they were incontestable; but most of what we know about Qusai, Abdul Muttalib, King Abraha, and the remarkable events of the Year of the Elephant was not written down until long afterward by Arab historians relying on hearsay. As with the Jews and many other ancient peoples, the Arab tradition of history was, for thousands of years, oral. It was a collection of tales told by old men around campfires beneath starlit skies; recitations that were memorized and handed down from generation to generation. No doubt, in the telling, truth was sometimes embellished with wonders; and when memory blurred, time translated history into legend. Yet behind the mists of legend the outline of truth can often be discerned.

Thus it was told that Arabs, Jews, and Arameans (the people of ancient Syria and Mesopotamia) were all cousins, for they were all descended from Noah's eldest son, Shem (the name from which the German historian A. L. Schlözer derived the term "Semitic" in 1781). Yet the word "Arab" does not appear in the tale of Noah or anywhere else in the book of Genesis; it first occurs in the second Book of Chronicles (17:11) referring to the nomads who wandered east of the River Jordan during the time of the Jewish King Jehosophat (c. 900–800 B.C.). Earlier stone-carved Assyrian and Babylonian inscriptions, however, refer to the "Aribi" or "Aribu" as the peoples of northern Arabia. Other traditions hold that the Arabs were descendants of the patriarch Abraham's son Ishmael, who lost his inheritance—the promised land of Israel—and wandered off into the desert.

Whatever their origins, there was no doubt that the Arabs inhabited one of the harshest environments known to man. Geographically Arabia may be said to consist of the overshoe-shaped peninsula that juts into the Indian Ocean between Africa and modern-day Iran. Almost all of this area except for the heel of the overshoe is barren. In the north, rolling plains of scrub brush afford some grazing, while to the south a great plateau shelves down from the Hejaz mountains to the Persian Gulf. Within this arid region are two huge seas of sand: the Nefood in the north and the grimly named Empty Quarter in the south. Rain is scarce anywhere in Arabia, but over these two dreadful wastes it almost never falls. Here and there, scattered over the peninsula like emeralds tossed upon a tan carpet, are oases— places of lush vegetation and lofty palm trees with wells fed by underground springs. Around some of these oases villages and towns grew—of which Mecca was one. As for the heel of the overshoe, the small area just opposite the Horn of Africa where the Red Sea meets the Indian Ocean, there abundant rainfall made agriculture and hence a settled civilization possible. Known to the ancient Hebrews as Sheba and to the Romans as Arabia Felix (Happy Arabia), this was the land of Saba from which King Abraha marched forth during the Year of the Elephant.

How could people live in the barren wastes that comprised most of Arabia? Harshly, precariously. In the extreme north they might find skimpy grazing for flocks of goats, but in most of the peninsula they subsisted on dates (called "the mother and aunt of the Arabs") gathered from palm trees at the oases, on the milk of the camel, and very occasionally its meat. But as we shall see, the camel had a far greater importance to Arab society than merely as a means of sustenance.

Arab survival in the desert depended on the solidarity and self-protection of the family, the clan (a group of related families), and the tribe (an association of clans). Such law as existed was based upon the responsibility of the clan or tribe for the acts of each of its members. An injury received by one individual

The Near East During Mohammed's Lifetime

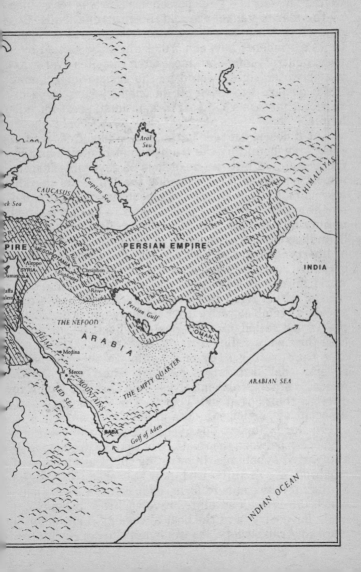

would be revenged by the whole clan or tribe, "life for life, eye for eye, tooth for tooth . . . burning for burning, wound for wound." Thus personal crime was restrained by the fear of vengeance and interminable feuds. But no such restraint prevented intertribal warfare. Sometimes arguments between tribes might be settled by a wise, neutral elder—but most often disputes over grazing or water rights would be the excuse for a *ghazu* (raid) designed to drive off an enemy's camels—a diversion that was a kind of Arab national sport for millennia.

But if desert life was harsh, it was also free. A man was honor bound by the traditions of his tribe and by public opinion but the vexations of government were almost nonexistent. The head of the tribe, the sheikh, was no more than a first among equals, usually bound by the council of tribal elders, who in turn governed mainly by example and exhortation. And besides, the boundless horizons, the vast skies, gave men a sense of liberty. Staring at night at the huge black canopy of stars overhead, the nomads imagined a natural world animated by free spirits like their own. These spirits, which lived in trees and rocks and wells and ancestral tombs, were either friendly—in which case they were called *jinn* (genies)—or hostile—in which case they were called *afrit* or *ghul* (ghouls). In either case they were worthy of worship. In their nomadic poverty the Arab tribes had only their voices with which to entertain themselves—and through which to develop their great art, poetry. The Arab language, innocent of particles, as the great Victorian orientalist Richard Burton observed, "Leaves a mysterious vagueness between the relations of word to word. . . . Rich and varied synonyms, illustrating the finest shades of meaning, are artfully used: now scattered to strike us by distinctness; now to form, as it were, a star, about which dimly seen satellites revolve." It is a language made for poetry, and the poet always held an honored place in Arab society. As the historian Ibn Rashid remarked in the eleventh century, "Whenever a poet emerged in an Arab tribe, the other tribes would come and congratulate it. Feasts would be prepared, and the women would gather together playing on lutes, as people do at weddings; men and boys alike would exchange the good news. For the poet was a defense to their honor, a protection for their good repute; he immortalized their deeds of glory, and published their eternal fame. On three things they congratulated each other— the birth of a boy, the emergence of a poet in their midst, or the foaling of a mare."

Unfortunately the genius of Arabic poetry is not translatable; its rhythm, rhyme, and subtlety are lost when confined within the more rigid discipline of English. And of course Bedouin poetry was meant to be recited aloud. But Arabic, like its kindred tongue Hebrew, has no written vowels—which is why, for example, you may find the name of the Prophet spelled out in English texts as Mohammed, Muhammed, Muhamad, Mohamet, or even Mahomat.

So with their hardships and freedom, their poetry and legends, the Bedouin tribes roamed their deserts in the Year of the Elephant as they had for ages past, happily secure from outside intrusion. That security— which preserved Arabia from conquest by Egypt, Assyria, Babylon, Persia, Rome, and all the other great empires of antiquity—was based, quite simply, upon the Arab monopoly of camels: no one else had them or knew how to use them. These strange, ungainly, ill-tempered creatures, capable of storing remarkable amounts of water in their systems, were the only animals able to survive in the deserts between far-flung oases. First domesticated by the Arabs around 1500 B.C., camels were employed by them not only as beasts of burden but also as personal transportation and, in battle, as cavalry steeds. No army unequipped with camels could hope to even penetrate the burning wastes of Arabia, much less subdue the camel-mounted Bedouin warriors.

Which was just as well, since in A.D. 570, the world beyond Arabia was dangerous, chaotic, and strife-torn. A century earlier (in A.D. 475) the western half of the once mighty Roman Empire had finally collapsed beneath the onslaught of various barbarian peoples, and its former provinces were now ruled by half-savage warrior tribes: Gaul (modern France) by the Franks; Iberia (modern Spain and Portugal) by the Goths; parts of Italy by the Lombards; North Africa by the Vandals. True, the eastern half of the old Empire survived— Greece, Asia Minor, Syria, Palestine, and Egypt were still governed by an Emperor from the great city of Constantinople (called Byzantium by its Greek inhabitants). But this Byzantine Empire was wracked by internal dissension between competing sects of the prevalent religion, Christianity. There were Coptic churches, Arian churches, Maronite churches, churches that adhered to the leadership of the all but powerless Bishop of Rome, and churches that looked for guidance to the Greek Patriarch of Byzantium. While the Byzantine emperors tolerated differences of faith within their domains, those subjects who did not adhere to the official orthodoxy of the state-protected Greek church were heavily taxed and from time to time viciously persecuted. Religious dissent, it was felt, weakened the Empire—and this was something the authorities in Byzantium could not afford, since along with all their other troubles they were engaged in a seemingly endless war along their eastern frontiers.

This age-old struggle, punctuated by occasional truces, was waged by the Byzantines against Persia. The ancient and mighty Persian Empire, ruled as an absolute despotism by its *Shah-in-Shah* (King of Kings), extended from western India through modern-day Iran and Mesopotamia into the Near East. It had been there for centuries, and for centuries it had hammered upon the approaches to the Mediterranean world. But behind its facade of timeless imperial power the Persian Empire, like the Byzantine, was afflicted with internal unrest. In Persia this dissension did not take on a religious character—Zoroastrianism (sun worship) was the official state religion, and those who did not profess it were simply killed out of hand. But in the domains of the King of Kings people groaned beneath the weight of a strict military dictatorship; rebellions were constant, and the fabled Peacock Throne itself was often usurped by military adventurers.

Echoes of the religious strife beyond their deserts had already been heard by the Arabs. Various Christian doctrines as well as Zoroastrianism had been brought to them by travelers, merchants, and refugees. Judaism too was known to the Bedouins, for after the destruction of Jerusalem by the Romans in A.D. 135 and the subsequent dispersion of the Jews throughout the Mediterranean world, many Jews had found sanctuary in Arabia. By the sixth century there were Jewish and Christian settlements in several desert towns. Zoroastrianism seems to have been transformed among a few of the nomadic tribes into the worship of al-Rahman (the sun)—a real if primitive form of monotheism. But the overwhelming majority of Arabs, while perfectly tolerant of these foreign religions, preferred their traditional animism (spirt worship). The strife of the outside world seemed no more threatening than a mirage on the distant desert horizon—and the nomadic tribes were content that it should remain so.

But the Bedouins were not to be exempted from the East-West confrontation of the sixth century—for both the Byzantine and Persian empires, the two superpowers of the day, were taking an ominously increased interest in Arabia.

The reasons for this were twofold. First of all there was the question of security. While the Byzantine-Persian frontiers from the Black Sea through Syria were fairly well defined by fortresses and battle lines, the boundaries of both empires simply faded out where they touched the northern Arabian deserts. From these unguarded regions both Byzantines and Persians were

vulnerable to raids and invasions. To secure themselves in this desolate area both sought allies among
the Arab tribes. Despite their tremendous military
might both empires feared these tribesmen, for they
could make sudden, commandolike assaults on Byzantine or Persian towns and trade routes, burning, killing, and looting with almost complete immunity; lacking camels, neither Byzantine nor Persian forces could
pursue the Bedouin raiding parties back into their desert strongholds.

The second reason for growing superpower interest
in Arabia was economic. The desert peninsula lay
athwart the sea trade lanes from India and the Far
East. Trading vessels, employing the monsoon winds
to sail between Bombay and the ports of Saba, carried
the spices, jewels, and silks of the Orient on the first
leg of their journey to the Mediterranean world. From
Saba this precious merchandise was transported by
camel caravan up the east coast of the Red Sea (thereby
avoiding the perils of those shark- and pirate-infested
waters) to Damascus, Alexandria, and other Byzan-
tine-controlled trading cities. To cut this profitable
trade route was in the Persian interest; it was in the
Byzantine interest to protect it.

Now perhaps we can more clearly perceive the solid
body of familiar human interests behind the legends
of the Year of the Elephant. For when King Abraha
marched north from Saba to attack Mecca, he was acting as an ally of the Byzantines, and despite his pro-
testations the Christian king's motives were far from
purely religious. The truth was that for many years
now the wealth and power of Saba had been in decline.
Although the vessels of the India trade still unloaded
at Sabaean ports, control of the vital caravan routes
to the north along the Red Sea coast had passed into
the hands of the merchants of Mecca. They, it seems,
were cleverly exploiting Arab religious feelings regarding their famous Kaaba to attract not only pilgrims but also merchants, traders, and commercial car-

avans. The great trade fairs of Mecca were draining off
too much wealth both from the Byzantine cities of the
north and from Saba itself. Furthermore, it was known
that caravans from Mecca often proceeded east to the
Persian Gulf. Thus much of the merchandise intended
for Byzantine use was being diverted to Persia.

By destroying the Kaaba, King Abraha hoped to put
an end to Mecca's attraction of pilgrim-merchants and
thereby regain for Saba control of the desert trade
routes. Thus King Abraha's expedition grew from commercial interests and in a larger perspective might be
seen as a minor incident in the continuing East-West
struggle for control of the Near East.

Minor perhaps to the great emperors of Byzantium
and Persia—but not to the citizens of Mecca or to their
leader, Abdul Muttalib. For having examined all possibilities, the Meccan Council mournfully concluded
that neither flight from King Abraha's huge host nor
resistance to it could preserve their Kaaba. But perhaps, despite his fearsome reputation, the Christian
invader might be open to negotiations. Abdul Muttalib,
at the head of a Meccan delegation, went out to meet
the Sabaean army when it was still some ten miles
from Mecca.

King Abraha received the delegation courteously.
He was not, he declared, a barbarian, but a Christian.
He had no desire to harm the city of Mecca or its inhabitants (after all, no matter who controlled the trade
routes, Mecca would remain an essential watering
place for the caravans) but only to destroy that abom-
inable temple known as the Kaaba, where false heathen
gods were worshiped. If the Meccans permitted him to
accomplish this task peacefully, then they and their
city would be spared. But if not, then Abraha feared
he might not be able to control his fierce soldiers. Who
could tell? They might utterly destroy the city and
massacre all its inhabitants.

The delegation returned to Mecca with heavy hearts.
They would by no means cooperate in the destruction

of their holy shrine, cost what it might. Abdul Muttalib advised all the people of the town to flee for refuge to the surrounding hills. No doubt many would perish of hardships—but none would be guilty of sacrilege. So the citizens of Mecca fled their city that night. Abdul Muttalib was the last to leave. Before he departed he leaned against the door of the Kaaba and prayed to God—not to the gods, but to God, which must have meant al-Rahman. He apologized for his inability to protect the temple and begged God to defend his own house of worship.

And God heard the old man's prayers. For a great miracle came to pass—that very night the great host of invaders was stricken with a terrible plague which would seem to have been smallpox. So swiftly and fatally did this disease spread among the Sabaeans that they immediately began a disorderly retreat, leaving the trail from Mecca south to Saba strewn with their dead. King Abraha himself died of this plague as soon as he got home. Maddeningly, history does not disclose to us the fate of the elephant.

Among the citizens of Mecca there was of course great rejoicing. They had no doubt that the Year of the Elephant would be remembered through all future ages for their miraculous deliverance. But in this they were mistaken. The Year of the Elephant (A.D. 570) was indeed to be remembered ever after—but not because of God's intervention on behalf of the Kaaba. Instead it was to be remembered as the year in which Abdul Muttalib celebrated the birth of a grandson named Mohammed.

CHAPTER TWO

Mohammed: The Birth of Islam

In the Name of God, the Compassionate, the Merciful
SAY: O ye Unbelievers!
....

I shall never worship that which ye worship,
Neither will ye worship that which I worship.
To you be your religion; to me my religion.

KORAN, CIX

When Mohammed was born (tradition fixes the date as August 20, 570), his father, Abdullah, was already several months dead. So the infant and his mother, who was herself a descendant of the family of Qusai, were taken into the household of Mohammed's grandfather, the revered Abdul Muttalib. But as it was the custom for children of the Quraish tribe to be farmed out to women of neighboring Bedouin tribes to be suckled and raised in the free air of the desert, the infant Mohammed was given over to the care of a woman of the Beni Saad tribe outside Mecca. It was not until he was six years old that Mohammed returned to his mother in Mecca—but within that same year she died, leaving him an orphan. Only a slave girl, Umm Ayman, remained to care for him. But of course there was also Abdul Muttalib, who was deeply attached to his grandson and lavished affection upon him. Then, when Mohammed was eight years old, Abdul Muttalib also died, leaving the orphan once again bereft.

Bereft, but not alone—for on his deathbed Abdul Muttalib had entrusted his little grandson to the care of another of his sons, Abu Talib, a member of the Beni Hashim clan, who was thus Mohammed's uncle as well as his foster father. Tribal feeling was far too strong to allow an orphan boy to be abandoned or neglected; and Abu Talib was an affectionate parent. But the succession of deaths of those nearest to Mohammed and the frequent change of households must have produced in him a feeling of insecurity and perhaps of loneliness. He was known as a pensive, introspective youth. But we have little record of Mohammed's early life beyond the fact that at the age of twelve he accompanied Abu Talib on one of those commercial journeys to Syria from which the Meccan merchant made his living, such as it was.

For Abu Talib, though kindly and generous, was far from wealthy, and his own children, who yearly increased in number, strained all his resources. The young Mohammed, feeling keenly his obligations to the household, earned what he could—sometimes through modest business transactions, most often as a shepherd. Serious and reserved, the young man soon gained a reputation for honesty and reliability. Then, when Mohammed was twenty-five, Abu Talib opened the door of opportunity to him.

Now it seems there was a wealthy and attractive widow in Mecca named Khadija. She was a woman of strong character and shrewd judgment who continued to manage with great success the business she had inherited from her late husband. This business included trading expeditions with camel caravans; and it appeared that the widow needed a reliable agent to accompany one of her caravans to the north, superintend the sale of her merchandise, and buy with the proceeds a consignment of Syrian goods for sale in

Mecca. Abu Talib talked Khadija into appointing Mohammed her agent on this venture.

The young man made the most of his opportunity in every way. Not only was the jorney to Syria a financial success, but so impressed was Khadija with Mohammed's qualities that a few weeks after his return to Mecca she proposed marriage to him. True, the widow was supposed to be forty years old, while Mohammed was only twenty-five—but she was sensible, attractive, wealthy, and of good family, being herself a descendant of Qusai. Mohammed accepted, and despite its apparently unromantic auspices their marriage proved to be a great success. Khadija bore her new husband two sons (both of whom died in infancy) and four daughters: Zeinab, Rukaiya, Fatima, and Umm Kulthum. Khadija's prodigious fertility would seem to indicate that like many Arabs of her day she was not really certain of her own age—she may well have been younger than forty.

With a devoted, wealthy wife who continued to manage her own business affairs, Mohammed was now freed from poverty and could indulge his taste for solitude and meditation—a taste that seemed to grow with age. Not that he was morose; with his family, as with congenial company, he could be humorous and even playful. Nor did he forget the debt he owed his uncle. To help relieve some of Abu Talib's expenses, Mohammed adopted one of the old man's sons, a six-year-old boy named Ali. Henceforth this youth was raised as if he were Mohammed's own. A further indication of Mohammed's kindness may be seen in the fact that shortly after taking Ali into his household he also freed and adopted a former household slave, a lad named Zeid Ibn Haritha who had been with Khadija since childhood.

It was now the year 610, and Mohammed, forty years old, grew more and more inclined to solitude and meditation. Leaving the hot, dusty streets of Mecca behind, he would often take refuge for days at a time in the caves of the hills around the city. Alone amid the black, rocky crags, he would brood about spirit worship, about the little he had heard of Judaism and Christianity, about the possibility of a single God, and about the life hereafter. When he returned home, troubled by his speculations, he would confide them to Khadija, who comforted and encouraged him, accepting his thoughts without question.

On one of these solitary vigils in the hills (it was in the month of Ramadan in the year 610), while sleeping in a cave on Mount Hira, Mohammed was visited by the Archangel Gabriel. "He came to me while I was asleep, with a coverlet of brocade, on which was some writing," Mohammed later declared. Four times Gabriel embraced him tightly and cried, "Read!" and each time Mohammed answered, "What shall I read?" Then the Archangel replied:

RECITE thou, in the name of thy Lord who created;— Created man from Clots of Blood:— Recite thou! For thy Lord is most Beneficent, Who hath taught the use of the pen;— Hath taught Man that which he knoweth not. . . .

KORAN, XCVI

The vision vanished, and Mohammed awoke full of fear. "I will go to the top of the mountain and throw myself down that I may kill myself and gain rest," he thought. But as he clambered up the mountainside, "while I was midway on the mountain," he later said, "I heard a voice from heaven saying, 'O Mohammed! Thou art the apostle of God and I am Gabriel.' I raised my head towards heaven to see, and lo Gabriel in the form of a man, with his feet astride the horizon."

Shattered by these visions, Mohammed hurried home and told Khadija everything that had happened. "Rejoice," she told him, "and be of good heart. I have hope that thou wilt be the prophet of this people."

Khadija believed in Mohammed's word unquestion-ingly—as did the rest of his family, including Ali and Zeid. And when shortly afterward Mohammed revealed his vision to his best friend, Abu Bekr, a man known among the Quraish for his honesty and intelligence, he too believed.

Thus Mohammed's first disciples were his own family and his best friend—the people who knew him most intimately in the entire world. And here we may well dispose of a slander propagated by some later commentators: namely, that Mohammed was an epileptic, given to fits that he misinterpreted as divine revelations and visions that were no more than the ravings of a disordered mind. Aside from the established fact that epilepsy is not a sign of madness and in no way affects rationality, there has never been any evidence to support the idea that Mohammed was afflicted with this disorder. The undisputed fact that those closest to him accepted his visions as perfectly genuine is powerful proof that they at least had no reason to doubt either his sanity or his honesty. To Americans, mostly raised in the Judeo-Christian religious tradition, the Moslem faith may seem in some respects strange, improbable. But to question the sincerity of Mohammed's inspiration is also to question the sincerity of Abraham, Moses, Jesus Christ, Buddha, and all the prophets and saints of all the world's great religions—for all these faiths rest on the word of God *as reported by man.*

At first Mohammed reported his visions only to close friends—and among these he recruited a small but devout following. But three years after Gabriel first spoke to him, the Archangel commanded that he go forth and preach to all mankind. So at the age of forty-three Mohammed went out into the public square before the Kaaba to announce God's word. The basic outlines of his creed were simple. God, he said, was One, Unseen, and All-Powerful; to portray him was blasphemy, to worship any other god or gods an abomination. Thus all the idols must be swept away and destroyed. As for

Mohammed, he was himself a messenger sent by God—
the latest of a line of God's prophets going back to
Abraham and including Moses and Jesus. He was ordered to warn men that there would be a day of judgment on which the dead would rise again. The wicked
would burn in everlasting hell, but those who acknowledged Allah (God) and his Prophet would enjoy the
bliss of eternal paradise. Mohammed knew these
things because they were told to him by the Archangel
Gabriel—sometimes man to man, sometimes through
an inner voice.

Mohammed himself declared that the basis of his
teaching was what he called the religion of Abraham—
ancient Judaism. But, claimed Mohammed, the pure
revelation made by God to Abraham had been much
distorted by the later Hebrews. Moses had attempted
without success to call them back to the true faith, and
eventually the prophet Jesus had been sent by God to
reclaim His children from error. But just as the Hebrews had adulterated the teachings of Abraham and
Moses, so too the Christians had distorted the teachings
of Jesus. Now, however, Mohammed had been called
by God to lead all men—Jews, Christians, pagans, and
sun worshipers—back to the truth they had either
never known or deserted. Mohammed did not regard
himself as the founder of a new religion but rather the
voice of the one eternal religion in which God willed
all men to believe. Although pagans, Zoroastrians, and
others were merely ignorant of God's Word, Jews and
Christians were heretics against it.

In general Mohammed's teachings seem to have
drawn more from the Old Testament than from the
New; he seems much more familiar with the stories
and teachings of the ancient Hebrews than with those
of the Christians. And through Mohammed's teachings
there seems to breathe the spirit of Jehovah, the wrathful God of the Old Testament. It is probable that Mohammed himself could not read—that what he knew
of the two older religions was hearsay. In any event

his versions of many Bible tales are often very different
from those related in Jewish or Christian scriptures.

Unlike the Bible, which records the story of the Jews
and the story of Jesus as told by men, Mohammed's
teachings copied down by his followers and later col-
lected into the Koran (the Recitation), are all the actual
words of God addressed to his Prophet. Throughout the
Koran revelations, statements, and commands are preceded by the word "SAY," the divine order to Mohammed to speak; for example:

> SAY: Verily, they who devise this lie concerning God
> shall fare ill.

or:

> RECITE to them the history of Noah, when he said
> to his people...

or:

> SAY: O men! now hath the truth come unto you from
> your Lord.
>
>   ALL FROM KORAN, X

And each sura (chapter)of the Koran is preceded by the
Prophet's authorization, as it were: *"In the Name of
God, the Compassionate, the Merciful."* Thus the actual
words of the Koran, written in the gorgeous, flowing
Arabic script, are themselves holy and worthy of ven-
eration. Through them men are to learn the will and
nature of God and submit themselves to that truth.
The religion of the Prophet is called, in Arabic, Islam,
which means "submission" to the will of God; those
who follow it are called Moslems, meaning "those who
submit."

One aspect of Islam that has often been ridiculed by
non-Moslems is the Prophet's very detailed description
of paradise. There, after death, the faithful are to re-
cline upon silken couches, devouring delicious fruits,
breathing perfumed air, surrounded by splashing foun-

tains and rivers of purest water, served by beautiful young boys and *houris* (maidens). Why all this should have provoked laughter among those who believed, for example, that after death they would sprout wings and fly around the heavens playing golden harps has never been clear. But, like the Christian version of heaven, the Moslem paradise was intended as an *allegory* of bliss eternal. It was described by the Prophet in just those terms that would be most meaningful to impoverished desert Bedouins. And the Prophet's promise that all who fell fighting for Islam would enter this paradise instantly and automatically was probably the single most powerful factor in promoting that Moslem battle fury which in a few decades was to conquer so much of the world. Arabs to this very day have been heard to shout, "Paradise, O Moslems, paradise!" as they go into action.

In spite of the obvious sincerity with which he preached, Mohammed's words fell upon largely hostile ears in Mecca. His command to purify the Kaaba by evicting its idols appeared to threaten the very basis of the Meccan economy—just as King Abraha's recent threat had done and for the same reasons. Besides, it was not pleasant for the citizens to hear that their age-old faith was mere superstition and that their ancestors were all roasting in hell. Mohammed's converts were few and his enemies many—but because he was a member of the powerful Beni Hashim clan of the Quraish tribe (who were thus honor bound to protect him), the Prophet and his family were safe from assassination. But not from insult. The children of Mecca made a sport of taunting Mohammed in the streets; the women of the town often tipped garbage onto his head from the roofs of their houses—one of them even scattered thorns outside his door to tear his feet when he went out barefoot. And among Mohammed's handful of followers there were some who could claim no clan protection at all. These were generally slaves (or ex-slaves whose freedom had been purchased by the generous Abu Bekr), and the Meccans did not hesitate to torture and even kill them. So desperate did the plight of these unfortunates become that in 615 Mohammed ordered them to flee Mecca, and with his own daughter Rukaiya, seek refuge in Christian Abyssinia.

Meanwhile the other Meccan clans of the Quraish decided to boycott the Beni Hashim clan so long as they insisted on protecting Mohammed. This meant no one would buy from, sell to, or even converse with them. But despite the fact that very few of the Beni Hashim believed in Islam, the clan refused to abandon their responsibilities. Yet the persecution in Mecca grew so bitter that Mohammed rarely went forth any longer to debate the old men who gathered daily in the square before the Kaaba.

Then in the year 619, the "year of mourning," both Mohammed's wife, Khadija, and his beloved uncle, Abu Talib, died. The Prophet was grief-stricken, and it may be that this personal sorrow was the final straw. Mohammed began to think now of emigrating to some other town perhaps more hospitable than Mecca. At first he thought of moving to the nearby hill village of Taif. But the people there mocked and snubbed him. "If you were sent by Allah as you claim," jeered one, "then your state is too lofty for me to address you; and if you are taking Allah's name in vain, it is not fit that I should speak to you."

So Mohammed turned his attention farther afield— all the way to the town of Yathrib, some three hundred miles to the northeast. Yathrib was not a commercial town like Mecca but an agricultural community in a beautiful oasis. It was inhabited by several rival tribes, of whom a few were Jewish. Possibly because the citizens of Yathrib had no vested interest in paganism (they had no Kaaba to protect), possibly because they were already familiar with many of Mohammed's precepts through their Jewish neighbors, the monotheism of the Prophet did not especially alarm them. In any event, during the annual month of pilgrimage to Mecca

Mohammed had an opportunity to discuss matters with some of the pilgrims from Yathrib. They assured him he would be welcome to their town, and a few even became converts to Islam. The Prophet, his hopes now centered on Yathrib, ordered his followers to slip out of Mecca in small groups, without ostentation, and make their way there. He himself remained behind with his adopted sons Ali and Zeid and his dearest friend, Abu Bekr.

But since the death of Abu Talib, whose influence among the Beni Hashim clan had held them to their duty to protect Mohammed, the Prophet's position in Mecca became daily more dangerous. Finally the elders of Quraish devised a scheme to murder him. Hearing of this, Mohammed went immediately to the house of Abu Bekr and announced, "Allah has given me permission to emigrate." So the two friends (followed later by Ali and Zeid) stole away from Mecca in the dead of night. For four days they hid in a cave in one of the hills near the city. At last Abu Bekr's daughter Asma came to the cave with three camels and a small parcel of food. She reported that the Meccans had put a heavy price on the heads of the two fugitives; they would pay one hundred camels for them, dead or alive. But with the aid of a Bedouin guide Mohammed and Abu Bekr successfully eluded pursuit and made their way to Yathrib. This was in the year 622, which is known to Moslems as the year of the hejira (migration) and is the starting point of the Moslem calendar. Yathrib had been known in ancient times by the Aramaic name *Medinat* (city), and Moslems were now to call it *Medinat al-Nabi* (City of the Prophet)—or Medina for short.

Despite the fact that Medina welcomed him as a refugee seeking asylum, Mohammed realized that he and his followers were in a precarious position there. At the Prophet's command some seventy Meccans had fled to Medina, leaving behind them all their worldly possessions. Besides these Emigrants, as they were called, there were about one hundred Medinan con-

verts, called Helpers. To weld these two groups together Mohammed decreed that each Emigrant should
be adopted by a Helper as his brother. A written charter
was drawn up for the little Moslem fraternity ordaining
that henceforth all true believers constituted a single
group, whatever their origins; every Moslem would
stand by every other to the death. Thus the powerful
hold of clan and tribal loyalties was now to be replaced
by religious solidarity.

A few weeks after their arrival in Medina Abu Bekr
purchased a derelict palm garden near the center of
the oasis. There the Moslems constructed a *masjid*
(mosque or place of prostration) in which five times a
day the faithful prostrated themselves in the direction
of Jerusalem while reciting *Allahu akbar* (God is the
most great) and other Moslem prayers. In these devo-
tions they followed the directions of an *imam* (leader);
but the *imam* was himself merely a worshiper—there
are no priests or other ecclesiastics in Islam.

Not long after arriving in Medina the Prophet married Aisha, one of Abu Bekr's daughters. By the time
of his death Mohammed had taken ten more wives.
These marriages were sometimes political alliances
with important clans and sometimes charitable, to provide a home for the widows and orphans of fallen followers. Polygamy had long been practiced in the Arab
world, partly as a social duty arising from the harsh
desert environment where widows and orphans not oth-
erwise protected might well starve. Later the Prophet
revealed in the Koran, "And if you fear that you cannot
do justice to orphans, marry such women as seem good
to you, two or three or four"—an injunction that has
since been read to *limit* the number of wives a man
may have to four.

There is no doubt that Mohammed's teachings in the
Koran raised the status of women in seventh-century
Arabia. Previously women had enjoyed no rights at all
and were looked upon as a burden on a tribe's economy;
female infants were often left to die of exposure. But

the Koran declared (Sura II) that women should enjoy the same rights as men in both marriage and divorce. It was the chauvinist interpreters of the Koran in later centuries who twisted its meaning to place women in subjection. Thus seclusion and the wearing of veils, originally intended to give women privacy and protection in a lawless society, became a form of imprisonment. And since Islam has no clergy, every man was priest and patriarch in his own household; a power men could exercise, if they wished, to dismiss wives at a whim. The threat of divorce, which is described in the Koran as "odious in the sight of God," thus became a powerful instrument of male tyranny.

It was in Medina that Mohammed revealed God's commands regarding family life, ethics, and the law. For example, the Koran prohibits all intoxicants and games of chance. Usury is likewise forbidden, as is the eating of pork. Many of the Koran's dietary laws, though somewhat less strict, are obviously derived from those observed by the Jews. Penalties were prescribed for stealing, murder, and other crimes. Slavery was permitted as an institution, but rigid limitations were placed on the rights of slaveowners, who are commanded to treat their slaves well. It will be noted that the Koran thus provided the first code of law in Arabia. Indeed, by replacing the old system of tribal vengeance with social rules of behavior it introduced the very concept of law to the desert tribes.

The early years in Medina were harsh with poverty for the Moslems—and the Prophet shared to the full the hunger of his followers. Years later Aisha recalled that the Prophet's household often passed weeks at a time without lighting a fire because they had nothing to cook. They lived on dates and water. To remedy this poverty it seemed only natural to the Moslems to engage in raids—and what better target than the caravans of the Meccan merchants who had so persecuted them? So when in January of the year 624 Mohammed learned that a caravan of one thousand laden camels was making its way south along the Red Sea on its return journey from Syria to Mecca, he decided to seize it.

Now this Meccan caravan was under the command of a man named Abu Sofian, a cunning, determined merchant who had been one of the Prophet's bitterest enemies in Mecca. Abu Sofian learned through spies that the Moslems intended to attack his caravan when it stopped at the oasis of Bedr to water. The merchant immediately dispatched a messenger to Mecca calling upon the inhabitants (almost all of whom owned some share in the caravan) to send out an armed force to escort him past the danger zone. But both Abu Sofian and the Moslems were much closer to Bedr than were the Meccans; so as a further precaution the caravan was rerouted on a detour well away from the oasis— with the result that the Moslems completely missed it.

But what Mohammed and his followers did find was the army of Meccans sent to foil them. This was a disagreeable, not to say fearful, surprise. The Moslems numbered but 314 poorly armed men, while the Meccan force numbered nearly one thousand well-equipped fighters. But the Meccans, having learned of the caravan's escape, saw little profit in fighting now. Furthermore, among the Moslems were Emigrants from their own city and from every clan in it; to kill them would be to break tribal tradition. Nevertheless, although a few Meccans declined to fight, the rest advanced upon the Moslems.

Mohammed and his followers fought with great fury—they had nothing to lose but their lives, and in doing so they would gain paradise. Nor were they restrained by those clan or tribal loyalties that had, for them, been replaced by religious faith. The halfhearted Meccans were no match for the Moslem fanatics, and despite their superiority in numbers and weapons they were soon routed. Bedr was the first of that string of victories through which Islam was destined to conquer half the civilized world within the space of a few decades.

But though they had won at Bedr, the Moslems had not after all plundered that caravan. Such spoils as they carried from the field—mainly armor, weapons, and camels—did little to assuage their continuing poverty. Accordingly, soon after the battle at Bedr Mohammed decided to despoil one of the Jewish tribes in Medina. His excuse for doing so was that the Jews, who had now become more familiar with the Prophet's teachings, utterly rejected Islam. So the Moslems besieged the Jewish tribe of Beni Qainuqa in their settlement until they surrendered. It appears that Mohammed's first impulse was to order their wholesale massacre; but certain Medinans interceded on the Jews' behalf, and in the end they were ordered to migrate to Syria, leaving behind them all their belongings, which were divided up among the needy Moslems.

While the Moslems of Medina were enjoying their newly plundered wealth, the merchants of Mecca were taking council. It was now apparent to them that they could no longer safely send their caravans along the coastal Red Sea route to the north, where they would be easy prey to Moslem raiders operating out of Medina. So it was decided that the annual fall caravan to Syria in 624 would be sent on a route east of Mecca through the Nejed country. Although this caravan was convoyed by a fighting force, the Moslems intercepted and captured it in its entirety; and a rich booty of silver and merchandise was brought back to Medina.

Now this interruption of their caravan trade was something the Meccans could not tolerate; commerce was the life blood of their city. Accordingly, in January of 625 Abu Sofian and a Meccan army of three thousand warriors advanced upon Medina to finally exterminate the insolent Moslems. Once again the Moslems were badly outnumbered and sadly underequipped; the Meccans had a cavalry of two hundred horsemen, for instance, while the Moslems had none. Yet once again

Moslem fanaticism made up for the inequality in numbers: the Moslems routed their enemies. But their victory was apparently too easily earned. For while the Prophet's followers were plundering their dead foes, the Meccans counterattacked and all but destroyed Islam then and there. Mohammed himself was badly wounded and like his followers had to seek refuge in a cave in the nearby hill of Uhud. From this sanctuary the Prophet was forced to watch the Meccans strip and mutilate his dead followers. When this had been accomplished, Abu Sofian himself advanced alone to the foot of the hill and shouted out to the cowering Moslems: "Today is in exchange for Bedr. War is like a well-bucket, sometimes up and sometimes down. . . . We shall meet next year again at Bedr." Then the triumphant Meccans mounted their camels and horses and rode slowly away.

If it seems strange to us that the Meccans did not pursue and kill Mohammed or ride into Medina (now completely defenseless) and utterly exterminate Islam, it must be remembered that to the pagan Arab tribes war had never been total. They fought for specific reasons—to protect a caravan route, to seize an oasis, to plunder a town—and when that objective had been accomplished, there was no reason to carry on a struggle. War was also waged to avenge tribal honor, and again, when it was deemed that an insult had been repaid, there was an end to the matter. The Meccans had, they thought, both avenged the honor lost at Bedr and taught the Moslems to leave their caravans alone; these goals achieved, they simply went home. They would eventually learn that to Mohammed and his followers war was neither a game nor a commercial enterprise; it was waged ruthlessly and totally, in pursuit of total ends. But by that time it would be too late.

Now victory in a religious war is always easily explained; God interceded on behalf of his worshipers. But defeat is another matter. To explain the defeat at Uhud Mohammed resorted to the same logic employed by Jewish prophets and Christian disciples—God had permitted the defeat to test the faith of his people. Nor did the Prophet allow the Moslems to brood about the disaster; he had much work with which to keep them busy.

This work consisted partly in the expulsion from Medina of the second of the city's three Jewish tribes, who were accused by the Prophet of having helped the Meccans. Whether true or not, this accusation sufficed to excuse the seizure of the homes and property of the unfortunate Jews. Another task for the Moslems was winning over the desert Bedouin tribes. Although it was true that the Medinans, like the Meccans, could field an army into the desert from time to time, the nomadic tribes who actually lived in that barren wilderness were the real key to its control. It was they who knew the trackless wastes and who could subsist there longer than any army; it was they who could, when and if they chose, raid the caravan routes and even close them down. Mohammed won the allegiance of the Bedouin tribes in the only meaningful way available—by sending out Moslem commando-type groups to raid them. Impressed both by the Prophet's military strength and by Moslem determination, the desert tribes came first to fear, then to respect the forces of Islam. And when they sent emissaries to deal with the Prophet, these often fell under the spell of Mohammed's powerful personality. Soon almost all the Bedouin tribes around Medina and even south toward Mecca had allied themselves with the Moslems. They were not at this time actually converted to Islam—they were simply in awe of it.

Nor did Mohammed cease preaching to the men of Medina, the majority of whom had already been won over to the new faith. And when certain powerful or influential men in the city refused to acknowledge the Prophet, they were assassinated. So Mohammed, using a judicious mixture of propaganda, murder, and military action, was waging a type of political war that would not be unfamiliar to us today. Against this campaign of primitive terrorism the Meccans were helpless. So little did they understand what was happening that they did not even bother to show up at Bedr in January 626 for the battle to which they had invited the Moslems a year earlier. The Moslems kept the appointment, however—and by doing so increased their prestige among the Bedouins.

Exasperated by their continual loss of influence and allies in the face of political methods they did not understand, the Meccans, led by Abu Sofian, decided to make an end once and for all of the Moslem community in Medina. For this purpose they raised an army of no less than ten thousand warriors—an immense force for that place and time—and in February 627 they advanced to the conquest of Medina.

Hearing of the huge army about to descend upon them, the citizens of Medina grew terrified—Moslems and pagans alike. But it so happened that there was among them a man named Sulman, a Persian convert to Islam, who had learned in his homeland some of the more advanced methods of warfare. He suggested that the city be defended by a wide ditch and a breastwork. All hands, including Mohammed, immediately turned out to dig, and within six days a deep trench girdled the town. It was completed just in time to prevent the Meccans from capturing Medina by assault.

This new technological development—a wide trench—completely baffled the Meccans. They complained that it was dishonorable and un-Arabic, but made no attempt to cross it. In fact they simply stared at it for twenty days; then, their rations growing scant, they abandoned the siege and melted away into the desert. They were hurried on their way by a howling gale.

Seeing his enemies thus dispersed, Mohammed wearily made his way home and prepared to take off his armor. But suddenly the Archangel Gabriel, mounted on a white charger, appeared before the Prophet and asked, "Have you already laid down your arms, O

Apostle of God? The Angels have not yet laid aside their arms, for God orders you to attack Beni Quraidha, and I am going on ahead of you." Whereupon Mohammed once again rallied his followers and led them to the camp of Beni Quraidha—the last Jewish tribe still living in the Medinan oasis. But this time the Moslems were not content with merely expelling their Jewish neighbors and stripping them of their belongings; at the Prophet's order every man of the tribe was killed and the women and children were sold into slavery. Before they were beheaded, the men of Beni Quraidha were offered the alternative of embracing Islam; but none did, and so all perished.

While many of the battles in which the Moslems engaged were forced upon them by their enemies, there is no use in attempting to justify the raids, murders, and massacres they carried out at the Prophet's command. Mohammed and his early followers lived in savage times, and they were men of their times. Murder and massacre were the accepted political weapons of Persians, Byzantines, Romans, Egyptians, Goths, Gauls—and Arabs too. Pagans, Christians, and Moslems alike employed the sword as the ultimate religious argument. Indeed, among his more bloodthirsty followers Mohammed's was often a voice of restraint and compassion. It may help us to understand, if not to condone, the violent fanaticism of the seventh century if we recall what hideous crimes have been committed in the name of twentieth-century ideologies.

About a year after the massacre of the Beni Quraidha the Prophet evidently felt that the prestige of Islam was sufficient for him to begin his final campaign against the Meccans. This time, however, the campaign would not be military, but rather peacefully political. It commenced when Mohammed reported a dream in which he had seen himself entering Mecca unopposed— to perform the traditional pilgrimage to the Kaaba. He proposed to obey this dream immediately, to the consternation of his followers, who were sure the Quraish would murder him on the spot. But, Mohammed pointed out, a peaceful pilgrimage undertaken during the holy month set aside by tradition for such visits could not be opposed by force. To break this tradition would not only blacken the name of the Quraish, it would also call into question the security of any and all pilgrims—thereby endangering the basis of Meccan prosperity. Although many of the Moslems remained unconvinced by this reasoning, some fifteen hundred of them, armed only with swords, accompanied the Prophet to Mecca early in 628.

Not far from the city they ran into a Quraish force sent out to prevent their further progress; but as Mohammed had predicted, this Meccan army offered them no violence. Negotiations were begun; and in the end the Quraish agreed that the Moslems might freely and peacefully enter Mecca to worship at the Kaaba—not this year, but the next. Mohammed's more fanatical followers were unsatisfied with this agreement. "Why not fight the Quraish? Why compromise thus?" demanded some. "You do what he [Mohammed] says," answered Abu Bekr mildly, "for I bear witness that he is the Messenger of God."

What Mohammed had accomplished by this frustrated visit to Mecca was the planting of the seed of an idea among the Meccans. For it now dawned upon the guardians of the Kaaba that if Mohammed himself looked upon pilgrimage to their shrine as a religious obligation, then perhaps the Kaaba would continue to enjoy the same prestige under Islam that it had among pagans. And so to accept Islam would in no way endanger Meccan commerce.

To drive home this point, in the following year (629) Mohammed and two thousand Moslems arrived at Mecca to visit the Kaaba as agreed. To the great relief of the Quraish the Prophet and his followers simply entered the famous shrine, touched the Black Stone, and made the seven ritual circuits of the temple, just as pagans had been doing for centuries. True, the Moslems ignored the heathen idols in the Kaaba—but this somehow no longer seemed so important. Combined with Mohammed's ever-increasing prestige, this demonstration that Islam would respect their Kaaba convinced many Meccans (especially the younger ones) that continued resistance to the new religion would be wasteful and foolish.

Mohammed waited yet another year to allow this lesson to percolate among the Quraish. Then in January of the year 630 the Prophet descended upon Mecca with ten thousand followers and accepted the peaceful unconditional surrender of the entire city. Its inhabitants now swore that there was no god but God and Mohammed was his Prophet. Before Mohammed's eyes the idols in the Kaaba were cast out and destroyed, as were the idols in all the private houses of the city. This accomplished, a general amnesty was proclaimed, and the Meccans vowed their allegiance to the Messenger of God. Victory, in the end, had been bloodless.

Mohammed himself did not remain in Mecca but returned to Medina. Delegates from the desert tribes and the towns and cities of Arabia came there in ever-increasing numbers to acknowledge his rule. Within eight years of the time he had fled Mecca as a hunted refugee with a price on his head, this remarkable man had raised himself to the overlordship of the entire Arabian peninsula. Well he might cry out during his last pilgrimage to Mecca in February 632: "O Lord, I have delivered my message and fulfilled my mission."

Having once again returned from Mecca to his home in Medina, Mohammed fell suddenly ill during the last days of May 632. He was then sixty-two years of age; and his symptoms, as described in Moslem tradition, would perhaps today be diagnosed as those of pneumonia. He suffered especially from severe headaches and a very high fever. By the tenth day of his illness the Prophet's condition had deteriorated alarmingly; his body was wracked with pain and he often lapsed into unconsciousness. But on the morning of the eleventh day (June 8, 632), supported by two attendants, he was able to attend the prayer service being held outside his house by Abu Bekr, who rejoiced to see his old friend apparently recovering. This effort, however, must have consumed the last of Mohammed's strength. He returned to his bed, a straw mattress on the floor, and while his wife Aisha bathed his forehead and wrists with cold water, he suddenly cried out. "O Lord, I beseech thee. Assist me in the agonies of death!" Then, his voice sinking to a whisper, he prayed, "Lord, grant me pardon. Eternity in paradise. Pardon." And with these words one of the most remarkable lives in the history of the world came to its end: Mohammed, Messenger of God, had passed into the presence of his Lord.

CHAPTER THREE

The All-conquering Faith

In the Name of God, the Compassionate, the Merciful
... And by Troops shall the unbelievers
be driven towards Hell, until when they reach it,
its gates shall be opened.
... But just is the sentence of punishment
on the unbelievers.

KORAN, XXXIX

It seemed at first that the death of the Prophet must inevitably lead to the death of Islam. For Mohammed had combined in his person the roles of God's messenger, supreme military commander of the faithful, and political ruler of all Islam—which at the time of his death meant almost all of Arabia. But he named no successors to any of these positions. Mohammed's overpowering personality had been the central axis around which Islamic unity revolved; with that axis removed it was to be expected that the scattered, newly converted, jealously independent Arab tribes would simply spin away into their traditional political and social anarchy. Islam did not yet even have the written Koran to hold it together, only scraps of the Prophet's sayings and the memories of his life.

But the Prophet had bequeathed something more than words and memories to his followers. For Islam, like Christianity and Judaism, was a liberating faith.

50

By unchaining people's minds from the superstitions of paganism it freed them also from fear of the natural world. As if awakening from a nightmare, people now perceived that their environment was not the capricious plaything of spirits and demons, but simple material reality obeying natural laws they might come to understand and even to manipulate. And by insisting upon the existence in all people of a God-given soul Islam gave to all of the faithful, no matter how humble their station in this world, an irreducible individual worth and dignity they had never before known. From this new understanding of human nature Islam had also developed a more just, more compassionate set of ethical principles to guide people's relations with one another. And finally, since Islam laid claim to universality, it provided its followers with an allegiance superior to the demands of family, clan, or tribe; Moslems now saw themselves as members of a far more extensive and potentially powerful human unity. In short, Islam had raised the consciousness of the faithful to a new and higher level of understanding from which they would not and could not retreat. It was not simply to attain paradise in the next world that Moslems would battle in the years ahead, but rather to defend and expand their comprehension of the world in which they lived.

To be sure, there was confusion and even apostasy immediately following the Prophet's death—yet these were resolved in a very short time. After the shock of their loss had abated, Mohammed's followers in Medina named Abu Bekr as *Kalifat rasul-Allah* (Successor to the Prophet of God, shortened in English to caliph). This appointment proved extremely wise; Abu Bekr was a man of much wisdom, humility, and common sense. He did not attempt to fill the Prophet's shoes. Knowing himself to be without military experience, he named Khalid ibn al-Walid, a former pagan military leader of proven ability, as supreme military commander of the Moslems. And rather than attempt to continue the tradition of divine revelation (as for example St. Paul did, years after Christ's death), Abu Bekr appointed a scholar named Zaid ibn Thabit to collect the Prophet's teachings lest they be forgotten. Zaid accomplished this task, gathering together the fragments of what would be the Koran "from date leaves and tablets of white stone, and from the breasts of men."

Thus Abu Bekr took the essential immediate steps necessary to preserve Islam. In a series of swift, stern military campaigns against those desert tribes who tried to reassert their independence, Khalid established the authority of the new caliph throughout all of Arabia in less than a year. And within that same period the scholar Zaid had gathered together and committed to writing the first Koran. This volume, which remained in Abu Bekr's possession during his lifetime, would become the basic text upon which later Moslem scholars would write their interpretations and commentaries; but the text itself was in existence within a year of the Prophet's death and was accepted as accurate by Mohammed's Companions (as all who knew him during his lifetime are called in Islamic tradition). Thus there would be no such argument over the Prophet's teachings as arose again and again over the teachings of Christ, whose utterances were not committed to a written gospel until nearly a century after his death.

Nor was Islam to be plagued, as other religions were, with false prophets. A few of these appeared soon after Mohammed's death—one at least had appeared during his lifetime. This man, named Musailama, had even been so bold as to write a letter to Mohammed that read: "From Musailama the Apostle of God, to Mohammed the Apostle of God: Let us divide the earth between us, half to you and half to me." Mohammed replied: "From Mohammed the Apostle of God, to Musailama the liar: The earth is the Lord's. He causes such of his servants to inherit it as he pleases." But after the Prophet's death Khalid made short work of all impostors, just as he did of apostates—and thereafter no false prophet could possibly stand against the majesty of the Koran.

With the unity of Arabia thus established and the authority of Islam unquestioned the new and dynamic Moslem nation began to look outward. There were compelling reasons for it to do so. First of all there was the need to find a new outlet for the martial spirit of the desert warriors: forbidden to make war on fellow Moslems or to practice on them their old sport of raiding, the tribesmen would have to find suitable enemies beyond Arabia. Then too there was an endless need for plunder, supplies, and fertile lands to alleviate the abysmal poverty of the Bedouins. Finally there was a new spirit of religious zeal to spread the word of the Prophet.

To Moslems as well as infidels the so-called Great Arab Explosion of the century following Mohammed's death—an explosion that toppled kingdoms and empires as if they were houses of cards—has seemed all but miraculous. That a relatively small group of impoverished desert tribesmen—lacking the skills and equipment of formal warfare, utterly without administrative experience or even much tradition of centralized political rule—was able to sweep professional armies before it, conquer well-fortified cities, and then establish an enduring, stable dominion over half the civilized world, remains an event without parallel in history. But as with all historical events there were good and sufficient reasons for this seeming miracle.

First of all we must ask, Who or what was to oppose the Arab conquests? The two superpowers, the Byzantine and Persian empires had been so long at war with each other that their resources in men, wealth, and, above all, morale were extremely low. And as we have seen, their subject peoples in Syria, Iraq, Palestine, Mesopotamia, Egypt, and elsewhere seethed with discontent. They had been taxed too heavily, exploited too cruelly, persecuted too harshly for their religious beliefs to feel anything but hatred for their foreign masters. In the West, beyond Byzantium, the Gothic kingdoms of Italy and Spain and the Vandal kingdoms of northern Africa were weak, ill organized, and imbued with a Christianity that had abandoned hope for this world in favor of the next. The world beyond Arabia in the seventh and eighth centuries was no more than a memory of vigor, a facade of power waiting to collapse at the first hard shove. The peoples suffering behind that facade would not fight desperately to preserve it.

But why, it may be asked, should the inhabitants of the Eastern empires and the Western kingdoms, no matter how disaffected, accept (and in some cases welcome) Arab rule? Why, in other words, should they substitute one set of foreign masters for another, one intolerant religion for another? Simply because the Arab yoke was very much lighter than what they were already used to. The new religion was not in fact intolerant. Islam accepted both Jews and Christians as people of the Book—misguided, heretical, but essentially related to the Moslem faith. Thus, though Christians and Jews might be forced to pay special taxes and barred from political or military positions, they were not to be actively persecuted unless they made war upon the faithful. And since in Moslem eyes all forms of Christianity were equally misguided, none of its many sects would be singled out for especially severe treatment—which, to the Copts of Egypt or the Monophysites of Palestine, for example, was a distinct improvement over the present situation.

As for pagans, who were still very numerous in Persia and the East, they would be forced to accept the Moslem religion. But in any case the basic precepts of the new faith were far superior both morally and philosophically to pagan beliefs. Nor was conversion terribly difficult. Islam, without priests, bishops, or hierarchy, is a religion of simplicity. The convert had only to declare his faith in Allah and Mohammed as his Prophet to make the basic profession required. Beyond this, good Moslems were expected to pray (facing Mecca rather than Jerusalem since Mohammed's death), give alms to the needy, fast during the holy month of Ramadan, observe a few simple dietary rules, and if health and wealth permitted, make the pilgrimage to Mecca at least once in a lifetime. These were the pillars of Islam, and their support was not a heavy burden.

It will be seen then that the great Arab conquests, though carried forward through battle, were not essentially military—they were political and ideological. Through their willingness to tolerate pluralistic societies the Arabs relaxed the tensions of older tyrannies. Very simply, Islam offered many peoples of the seventh and eighth centuries a freer, more secure, more peaceful life than they had recently known—and that was the ultimate secret of its success.

The expansion of the infant Arab caliphate began when Abu Bekr ordered Khalid to make a series of probing raids into Byzantine Syria in 634. The object was two-fold: to secure plunder and to bring local Arab tribes into submission to Islam. The Byzantine Emperor Heraclius, astonished by the sudden emergence of this threatening new power from the arid deserts, sent an army to protect Damascus; it was decisively defeated by Khalid's forces in the battle of Ajnadayn on July 30, 634.

One month later Abu Bekr died. He was succeeded without much argument by Omar ibn al-Khattab, a man of severe and autocratic temperament. The Arab advance was unaffected; Khalid's forces finally captured Damascus in 636 and Jerusalem fell to Caliph Omar himself in 638. The following year all of Syria came under Arab rule.

While Arab armies were driving the Byzantines out of the Near East, other Islamic forces developed their raids against Persia into a full-scale invasion. They defeated the main Persian army at Kadisiya in the summer of 637, then went on to capture the Persian

The Great Arab Conquests

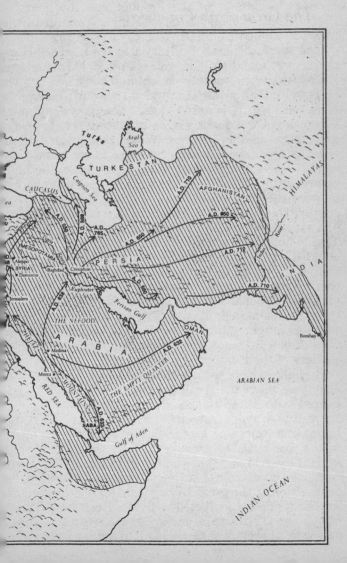

capital of Ctesiphon on the Tigris River; all of Iraq fell into their hands. Over the next ten years the Arabs carried the banner of the Prophet into the heart of Persia itself; the last King of Kings, Yazdajird, was killed as he fled from the Arab cavalry in 651.

The secret of Arab military success in these campaigns was mobility. The well-mounted, lightly armed Arabs (they carried only spears and bows and arrows along with their swords) would charge down on enemy lines until within javelin range. Then they would hurl their spears and shoot flights of arrows, wheel away, and make another charge. When they judged their enemies weakened enough by these maneuvers, they would close in for the kill. Used to living off the land wherever they went, Arab forces were not encumbered, as were the Byzantines and Persians, by slow-moving supply trains, sluggish army administration, intricate and vulnerable webs of communication and command. Tied to no lines of supply or command, the Arabs could strike anywhere. Sometimes they would bypass enemy armies to disrupt their rear-area bases, disappear, and then, yelling, *"Allahu akbar,"* come charging down on an exposed flank. Furthermore, convinced that death in battle meant instant entry into paradise, the Moslem warriors fought with reckless, furious bravery; man for man they were much more than a match for any other soldiers of their day.

And as we have seen, resistance was not strong. For example, when the Arab general Amr ibn al-As appeared with three thousand cavalry at al-Arish on Byzantine Egypt's eastern frontier in A.D. 639, the Egyptians welcomed him. Some resistance was made in the great city of Alexandria, but within a year it and all the rest of Egypt had fallen to Islam. For many centuries it was said that Caliph Omar had ordered the destruction of the great library in Alexandria because "either its books conflicted with the Koran and therefore ought to be burned, or they agreed with the Koran and were therefore superfluous." In actual fact the famous library at Alexandria had been destroyed much earlier—in the third century A.D. during a civil war in the time of the Roman Emperor Aurelian. The myth that the Arabs destroyed it was a lie invented by thirteenth-century Christian propagandists. In fact, the burning of books, the destruction of centers of learning, were absolutely contrary to Islamic doctrine and tradition. One of the best-known sayings of the Prophet is, "The ink of the scholar is more sacred than the blood of the martyr."

By the middle of the seventh century, then, Islam had already conquered an impressive empire: all of Arabia, all of the Near East except Asia Minor, all of Persia, all of Egypt—and Arab raiding parties were already probing across the Libyan desert to the West and into India in the East.

How could the loosely disciplined, illiterate desert warriors administer so vast a domain inhabited by such diverse peoples? They didn't try—at least not in detail. The Arab commanders, often accompanied by converted Persian, Christian, or Jewish political advisors, would depose or kill the very highest local rulers—but administration of conquered territory was left largely in the hands of the already established local bureaucracy. After gathering their initial plunder, the Arabs would establish garrisons on the edge of the desert and impose taxes on the subject population. So long as local officials faithfully gathered and paid these taxes (they were generally light), conquered peoples were left pretty much to their own devices. As has been pointed out, Arab rule was racially and religiously tolerant; far from imposing their customs on the conquered, the Arabs held themselves aloof. They constituted a kind of warrior master race to which not even Moslem converts were admitted. These converts were exempted from certain taxes but like Christians and Jews were *subjects* of Arab rule. Later of course, after Arabs had intermingled with local populations through marriage, these distinctions between Moslems would disappear;

but at the time of the great conquests the Arabs remained an exclusive elite.

Perhaps the most remarkable aspect of all this was the way powerful Arab generals, commanding mighty armies and ruling huge areas, continued to accept without question the ultimate authority of the caliph living in far-off Medina. For instance, after Amr ibn al-As had conquered Egypt he received a letter from the Caliph Omar in which he was accused of not sending a proper share of the booty back to Medina. "My suspicion has been aroused against you, and I have sent Mohammed ibn Maslama to divide with you whatever you possess," the caliph wrote. And when the caliph's auditor arrived to seize part of Amr's loot, the mighty general merely complained, "An age in which the caliph treats us in this manner is certainly an evil age. Before you came I wore brocade robes with silk borders." "Hush," replied Mohammed ibn Maslama, "had it not been for this age of the caliph which you hate, you would today be bending in the courtyard of your house, at the feet of a goat, whose abundance of milk would please you or whose scarcity would cause you dismay." Amr ibn al-As thought upon this and then exclaimed, "I beg of you for God's sake not to report what I have just said to the caliph. A conversation is always confidential." Mohammed smiled. "So long as the caliph Omar is alive I shall mention nothing that has passed between us." By such moral authority the Caliph Omar, a bent old man who habitually wore a ragged cape and lived in a tiny desert town, ruled a mighty empire.

But in November 644 the Caliph Omar was assassinated by a Persian slave. A special council of elders appointed as caliph Othman ibn Affan of the powerful Umayyad clan of the Quraish tribe (he was also a son-in-law of Mohammed, having married in succession two of the Prophet's daughters). This choice displeased the followers of Ali, Mohammed's adopted son, who felt that their candidate was the natural successor, but they accepted the council's decision.

Unfortunately Othman proved to be a weak and vacillating caliph. He was unable to maintain the disciplined authority established by Omar. Discontented tribesmen in the Hejaz Mountains rose in revolt, and in June 656 Othman was murdered while at prayer in his house in Medina. Now surely, thought the supporters of Ali, their leader would be chosen caliph. But Ali was opposed by Othman's relatives of the Umayyad clan—who included his nephew Muawiya, the governor of Syria—as well as by the Prophet's widow Aisha and several of the Companions. The argument could only be decided by force; and in December 656 Ali was victorious at the Battle of the Camel, fought near Basra and so called because Aisha, "Mother of the Faithful," rode a camel at the heart of the fighting. Ali's followers now named him caliph and transferred the capital from Medina to Kufa.

But Ali's triumph was short-lived. Although he was pious, brave, and a good general, Ali was a poor statesman. Muawiya, with the support of Amr, conqueror of Egypt, gathered an army and rose in revolt, demanding vengeance for the murder of his uncle, Othman. Ali led forth his troops to meet the rebels at the battle of Siffin (July 657); but just when it appeared he was winning, Ali was defrauded of victory. For the clever Amr ibn al-As conceived the idea of sending his reserves into the struggle with copies of the Koran fixed at the tips of their spears, as if calling upon Allah to decide the issue. The more pious among Ali's followers immediately insisted that the fighting stop. Both sides agreed to arbitrate their differences—and the decision went against Ali. He refused to accept this verdict, but by then many of his soldiers had deserted him. Ali had no choice but to retreat to his capital at Kufa, where in January 661 he was himself assassinated. By that time Muawiya had proclaimed himself caliph and established his capital in Damascus.

But there were many who continued to revere Ali and his descendants as the true caliphs while regarding Muawiya and the Umayyads as mere usurpers. They became known as Shias (partisans) of Ali, as opposed to Sunnis (orthodox)—the majority of Moslems. This split became and remains the great schism in Islam; of five hundred million Moslems in the world today, some fifty million are Shias.

Muawiya proved himself an able commander of the faithful and a good administrator. But the two great projects of his caliphate, the conquests of North Africa and the Byzantine Empire, were destined to fail. Having driven the Byzantine forces from Syria, the Arabs had for some years been trying to break through the Taurus Mountain barrier onto the plateau of Asia Minor (present-day Turkey). In this they were unsuccessful, partly because the mountain passes were well garrisoned with Byzantine troops ensconced in fortresses, partly because the Arab warriors were unused to the intensely cold winters of that region, and partly because Arab tactics were simply unsuited to mountain warfare. Although during the summer they sometimes raided into Asia Minor, the Arabs could not maintain themselves there.

Since the land approaches to Byzantium itself, both through Asia Minor and the Balkans, were heavily defended, the key to its conquest lay in sea power. Caliph Othman had seen this and had organized an Arab fleet, which had raided the islands of the eastern Mediterranean and even defeated the more experienced Byzantines in two sea battles. Muawiya expanded Othman's fleet and used it to seize the island of Cyprus. If it seems strange that the tribesmen of landlocked central Arabia should prove such brilliant sailors, it must be remembered that they had been navigating the ocean of sand for centuries.

In the year 670 Muawiya decided to assault the great Byzantine capital city directly. His fleets now were powerful enough to sail unscathed through the Dardanelles, and the Arab warriors had by this time acquired some skill in siege warfare. Yet their project was daring. The great walls of Byzantium had withstood the attacks of barbarians and of Persians for decades at a time; their ramparts were of great height and solidity. Furthermore, the Byzantines—no longer fighting in defense of distant, half-hostile provinces, but for the last refuge of their country, their religion, and their wives and children—put up a furious fight. Day after day the assaulting Arab lines beat in vain against the towering walls—only to be driven off, sometimes by the frightening Byzantine secret weapon, Greek fire. For seven years Islam besieged Byzantium, until at last Moslem losses in men and treasure proved too great to sustain.

This defeat saved all of Europe from Arab conquest, for beyond the walls of Byzantium there existed no force that could possibly have resisted the armies of the faithful. During all the Dark Ages of Europe's decline, the Byzantines kept shut the continent's Eastern gate. When at last, in the fifteenth century, the city fell to the Ottoman Turks, Europe was ready to defend itself.

While besieging Byzantium in the east Muawiya had also sent Arab forces probing west along the shores of North Africa. This area, comprising today the nations of Tunisia, Algeria, and Morocco, had been ruled in turn by Phoenicians, Carthaginians, Romans, and Vandals, and at the time of the Arab conquests was part of the Byzantine Empire. The people of the coastal cities such as Carthage were Latin-speaking Christians, but the deserts and mountains south of the coastal region were the domain of wild, pagan tribes of Berbers. These warlike people of mysterious origin had dominated the North African hinterland for more than a thousand years. They spoke a Semitic language closely related to Arabic, and like the Arabs they were hardy and adept at desert warfare. They had never been subdued by Romans, Byzantines, or anyone else, and they saw no reason to bow to Islam.

Arab forces in North Africa were commanded by Uqba ibn Nafi, nephew of the great Amr ibn al-As, conqueror of Egypt. Uqba, a dashing, adventurous cavalryman, correctly diagnosed the reason for previous Arab failure in North Africa as a lack of secure bases from which to attack and dominate that vast region. Accordingly he advanced across present-day Tunisia to an area south of Carthage and there laid out an Arab military camp, which would one day grow into the great city of Kairouan. The coastal cities offered little resistance to the Arabs—but the Berbers of the interior were a different matter. To subdue them, in the year 681 Uqba led an Arab army from his base at Kairouan fifteen hundred miles across North Africa into Morocco (then still known by its Roman name, Mauritania). He captured the city of Tangiers and then marched down the Atlantic coast to the site of present-day Agadir. There, it is said, he rode his horse into the water, waving his sword and crying out: *"Allahu akbar!"* If my course were not stopped by this sea, I would still ride on to the unknown kingdoms of the West, preaching the unity of Allah, and putting to the sword the rebellious nations who worship any other god but him!"

A breathtakingly daring raid—but not a conquest. For the entire area through which Uqba's men had ridden was still in the hands of the Berbers. These, under the leadership of thier great chief, Kusaila, fell upon the Arab columns as they returned east, and in 683 they killed Uqba and all his men at the battle of Tahuda (near present-day Biskra in Algeria). Thereupon Berbers all over North Africa rose in revolt, and the Arabs soon found themselves expelled from even the coastal cities and once again forced back to the gates of Egypt.

Meanwhile Muawiya, ruling from his capital city of Damascus, devoted himself to administrative reforms, which were to prove more enduring than his abortive, overextended conquests. The basic problem was starkly simple: there were not enough pure-bred Arabs to conquer and rule the world. Furthermore, the accumulation of loot, slaves, wives, and wealth was eroding Arab fighting qualities; the hardy desert warriors were growing fat and losing their puritanical fervor. Many had settled in cities and towns, becoming landed gentlemen—and there was a steady, growing fusion of Arabs with their subject peoples. Under the circumstances a regular governmental administration was necessary. And, given the lack of manpower, the older exclusive master-race attitudes would have to change. So under the Caliph Othman infidels who converted to Islam had been recruited to administer conquered territory; under Muawiya such converts enjoyed even greater acceptance and were permitted to join the active Arab fighting forces.

During the caliphate of Muawiya the first police forces were formed in Kufa and Basra (in present-day Iraq). Judges, treasurers, and city officials as well as governors were appointed in all provinces. Muawiya also established a postal service and attempted to regularize finances. This last project was difficult, for treasury officials in Egypt kept their accounts in Coptic, those in Syria kept them in Greek, those in Persia kept them in Farsi. The language problem was growing acute; if the Arabs wished to remain in control of their empire they would have to become educated. Yet despite the Prophet's praise of scholarship the desert Bedouins continued to regard book learning as somehow effeminate.

But of all the problems faced by the Caliph Muawiya the most vexing was that of a successor. As he grew old in years, Muawiya advanced the claims of his own son, Yezeed. But this young man had a reputation for vice, impiety, and foolishness. Furthermore, in attempting to establish a dynasty Muawiya was going against the teachings and spirit of Islam—not to mention tribal tradition. So when Muawiya died in the year

680 and Yezeed was proclaimed caliph in Damascus, a bitter civil war immediately erupted. The various tribes and clans, centered around Medina, Mecca, Damascus, and Kufa, fought to impose their own candidates as caliph. The struggle was prolonged, complicated, and bloody; at its worst it degenerated into an anarchy that threatened the very existence of the Arab Empire. Eventually in the year 685 Abdul Malik ibn Merwan, a member of the Umayyad family, was named caliph in Damascus. But it took him another six years of fighting to subdue rebellions before he became undisputed master of the whole Arab Empire in 692.

With civil disturbances at an end the new Caliph Abdul Malik once again turned the energies of Islam to foreign conquest. Campaigns were waged against the tribesmen of present-day Afghanistan, and Arab forces penetrated further into India. In the West a large Arab army from Egypt under the command of Hassan ibn Naaman advanced once again across North Africa in 695. This Arab host captured Carthage and, like the Romans centuries earlier, razed the city to the ground—this time so throughly that it has never been rebuilt. But although, like Uqba before him, Hassan could conquer the coastal plain, he could not subdue the Berber tribes of the interior. The most prominent of these tribes, the Zenata Berbers, had only recently emerged from the Atlas Mountains. According to ancient Arab historians the Zenatas were converts to Judaism and led by a woman known to history only as the Kahina (prophetess). The Zenata fell upon the Arabs at Tebessa (in present-day Algeria) and utterly routed them—Hassan barely managed to escape to Egypt with a remnant of his forces.

Undeterred, Caliph Abdul Malik reinforced Hassan with a powerful new army and in 702 ordered him to resume the offensive. Meanwhile the Kahina had ordered her followers to utterly destroy the cities, towns, orchards, and fields of the coastal plain. The Arabs came only to conquer these, she said, and if they no

longer existed the Zenata would remain unmolested.
This policy, however, turned the inhabitants of the
coastal plain against the Berbers, so that when Hassan
led his new army once again to the West, he found
important new allies among the Greek- and Latin-
speaking populations. The Arabs fought a great battle
with the Zenata Berbers at Tabarca near the ruins of
Carthage; the Zenata were completely defeated, the
Kahina killed. Thereafter almost all the Berber tribes
acknowledged Islam, and the Arab conquest of North
Africa became permanent. To replace Carthage Hassan
built up a nearby village named Tunis, which remains
today the capital of Tunisia.

In 705 Hassan was removed from his post as governor of North Africa and replaced by Musa ibn Nusair.
Caliph Abdul Malik had died in October of that year;
and his son, Waleed ibn Malik, the new caliph, probably preferred to appoint his own man to so important
a position. Musa set himself the task of consolidating
the conquests of his predecessor, and from 705 to 708
he marched his army across North Africa, taking Tangiers and subduing the Atlantic coast of Morocco. All
of North Africa was now securely in Arab hands—and
the converted Berbers soon proved themselves even
more enthusiastic Moslems than their Arab conquerors. Thus after thousands of years North Africa—which
had always been an extension of European civilization,
the southern shore of that Roman "lake" (the Mediterranean Sea) that was the center of the Western
world—passed from European rule and culture. Despite the incursions of nineteenth-century imperialism
it was never to return.

Now when Musa subdued the North African coast,
the one city that he could not conquer was Ceuta (in
present-day Morocco), a Byzantine colony across the
narrow straits from Spain, ruled by one Count Julian.
Since Byzantium was far away, Julian relied for aid
upon the Gothic rulers of Spain, to whom in any case
he was related by marriage. Either because he felt that

his in-laws had not given him sufficient support in his defense of Ceuta or for more obscure reasons (it is said that the Gothic King Roderic had seduced his daughter), Count Julian entered into correspondence with Musa. He proposed to the Arab commander that they make a joint invasion of Spain, offering to supply the ships necessary for such a venture. Musa reported all of this to Caliph Waleed, who—rather reluctantly—authorized a reconnaissance.

Accordingly, in July 710 Musa sent a force of some four hundred men across the straits in Count Julian's ships. Landing near Algeciras, the Moslems plundered the neighborhood and then returned to Africa. Encouraged by the results of this raid, in April 711 Musa sent a force of seven thousand warriors (mostly Berbers) to Spain under the command of one of his household servants, a converted Berber named Tariq ibn Zayyad. Tariq established his headquarters on a gigantic rock overlooking the straits which has ever since borne his name: Jebel al-Tariq (Mountain of Tariq) or, in English, Gibraltar. Once this Moslem beachhead had been secured, Musa dispatched another five thousand men to reinforce Tariq's army.

Meanwhile the Gothic King Roderic had gathered his forces together and was advancing south. Goths and Moslems met in July 711 at the battle of Wadi al-Bekka a few miles east of Cadiz. Roderic—betrayed, it is said, by several of his subordinates—was utterly defeated, and was himself killed in the fighting. The victorious Tariq immediately followed up the battle with an advance to the north. Moslem columns captured the cities of Cordova and Elvira, while Tariq himself led the main body straight to the Gothic capital at Toledo, which fell without a struggle. In the following year (712) Musa arrived from North Africa with a new army that captured Merida and Seville and by the summer of 713 reached the Pyrenees Mountains in the north. All of Spain and present-day Portugal, with the exception of a small mountainous area of Galicia on the Bay of

Biscay, had fallen to Islam in the space of three years. The Moslem capital was established at Cordova and the country became known as al-Andalus.

The swift Arabic, or perhaps we should say Berber, conquest of Spain, like other victories of Islam, has seemed nothing short of miraculous to later observers. But the same social and political conditions that had facilitated the Arab conquests elsewhere were also operative here. The Goths, who had supplanted the Romans as masters of the peninsula and had adopted Christianity, were harsh taskmasters. Holding themselves aloof from the general population, they ruled Spain as a continuous exercise in plundering. Almost all the unhappy inhabitants of their kingdom were slaves or serfs who had no love for Gothic rule. And the usual religious persecutions of differing Christian sects and of Jews were commonplace. The people of Gothic Spain, like people elsewhere, looked upon the Moslems more as liberators than as conquerors—and, as elsewhere, Arab rule proved light, intelligent, and above all tolerant.

As for Musa and Tariq, they were summoned back to Damascus by the Caliph Waleed. But Waleed died in February 715, before the two conquerors arrived; his brother, Sulaiman, who now became caliph, carried out the dead man's will. Musa was imprisoned, flogged, fined, and banished to die in poverty and obscurity, while Tariq was condemned to return to his old employment as a household servant. Like Waleed, Sulaiman had no intention of permitting any of his commanders to reap a glory that might make them popular rivals for the caliphate itself.

Under Sulaiman Arab armies subdued Afghanistan, central Asia to the northern limits of the Caspian Sea, and much of northern India. They also advanced partway across Asia Minor and again unsuccessfully besieged Byzantium. Meanwhile, far to the west, Moslem forces in Spain—commanded now by the Arab Governor Abdul Rahman ibn Abdulla—had breached the line of the Pyrenees and were raiding into southern France. In 718 the Moslems captured Carcassonne and Narbonne, besieged Toulouse, and raided into Burgundy. It seemed that France might suffer the same fate as Spain.

In the eighth century "France" really meant the kingdom of the Franks, the barbarian tribe from across the Rhine who had supplanted the Roman rulers of Gaul during the fifth century. But this kingdom of the Franks was itself practically a fiction, for the Frankish tribes had not created a nation-state such as we would recognize. They had carved Gaul into baronies, principalities, and dukedoms that owed only a shadowy, formal allegiance to the line of Frankish kings. These kings (of the Merovingian dynasty founded in 481 by Clovis) had degenerated to such an extent that they were no longer masters even in their own homes, that function having been usurped by a series of so-called Mayors of the Palace. So when the Moslems advanced deeper into "France," they were opposed only by local forces. In 725 the armies of Abdul Rahman raided into the Rhone valley; in 732 they besieged Bordeaux and ravaged all the countryside as far as the River Loire. It was then that the sorely pressed Eudes, Duke of Aquitaine, sent a desperate appeal for help—not to the king of the Franks, but rather to his Mayor of the Palace, Charles Martel.

Martel gathered an army and advanced south to relieve Aquitaine; his forces ran into the main Moslem army near the city of Tours. There the Franks and the Moslems fought a bloody pitched battle in October 732. After heavy fighting Abdul Rahman was killed and his army driven from the field. But so heavy had been the Frankish casualties that Charles did not pursue his beaten foes with any great vigor. For another twenty years the Moslems were to raid and rule parts of southern France until finally they were driven back behind the barrier of the Pyrenees. Nonetheless the Frankish victory at Tours was to mark the extreme limit of Islam's advance into Western Europe. Charles Martel, known now as "the Hammer of Tours," established himself as King of the Franks—and his descendant Charlemagne would one day carry the banner of Christendom over the mountains into Spain itself.

One of the most fascinating "ifs" of history remains the question, What if the Moslems had won at Tours? Would they then have advanced all the way to the English Channel? Would they have wheeled south to conquer Italy from the north or Byzantium from the west? There exists some evidence that Abdul Rahman had considered these possibilities. In that case would all of Western Europe have fallen to Islam, with incalculable consequences? Or was a Moslem defeat at Tours or elsewhere north of the Pyrenees somehow inevitable?

The immediate reasons for the Moslem retreat from France are fairly apparent. Their lines of communication and reinforcement from Spain were too long and too perilous—subject to the same kind of guerrilla attack the Arabs had once employed against Byzantine and Persian supply lines. Furthermore, northern climes were uncongenial to African and Near Eastern warriors, who were unprepared for campaigning in the cold and snow. But the underlying reasons for Islam's failure to conquer Western Europe were not military— they were social and ideological.

For more than a century now the Arabs in both the Near East and North Africa had been enjoying the fruits of their conquests. They had been succumbing to the ease and pleasures of a settled way of life. They were no longer hardy Bedouin warriors but, for the most part, sophisticated, comfortable rulers and administrators. As we shall see, the armies of Islam were increasingly recruited from recently subdued and converted border peoples—in the East from among the Turks of central Asia; in the West from among the Berbers of North Africa. But as these fierce tribes began in turn to adopt the easier, more settled, more civilized life now opened to them, they—like the Arabs before them—lost much of their zeal for conquest and hence their fighting edge. And in Western Europe these less than enthusiastic soldiers came up against Franks, Normans, and other semi-barbaric warrior tribes whose military virtues had not yet been eroded by the comforts of civilization.

Perhaps of even greater importance was the fact that while Islam had appeared as a liberating doctrine to the peoples of the Near East and Africa groaning under the Byzantine and Persian tyrannies, it did not so appear to the people of Western Europe. The Franks, for example, were suffering under no foreign domination, nor did they intend to accept that status from Moslems or anyone else. Furthermore, while the vitality of Christianity in the Near East and Africa had been undermined and eroded by endless sectarian persecutions, in Europe it was still a highly dynamic force, liberating its recently converted barbarian tribes just as Islam had once liberated the Arab Bedouins. And like the earlier followers of the Prophet, the Christians of Europe would fight to the death to preserve their newly raised consciousness. It seems safe to say that a Moslem conquest of Europe was never a very real possibility.

But despite that inevitable setback, consider the amazing achievement of the Arabs: in just one century the ragged desert followers of an impoverished Prophet who had died in an obscure Arabian village had carved out one of the world's greatest empires. The domain of Islam stretched from the Pyrenees to the Himalayas, from the Atlantic to the Indian Ocean, from central Asia to central Africa. Not only had the Arabs conquered this huge area, but they had remained to govern it—and were in the process of creating within it a culture that was to prove permanent. In all of recorded history their accomplishment remains unique.

CHAPTER FOUR

The Golden Age

In the Name of God, the Compassionate, the Merciful
...And God gave them the recompense of
this world, and the
excellence of the recompense of the next.
For God loveth the doers of what is excellent.

KORAN, III

It was around the beginning of the ninth century that Islam's Golden Age began—those fabulous years celebrated in *The Thousand and One Nights* that have aroused the wonder and delight of countless generations ever since. It was the time of splendid kings and cunning viziers, of powerful magicians and wise philosophers, of gallant knights in the gardens of Spain, of magic carpets and flying horses soaring over the rooftops of fabled Baghdad, of harems and eunuchs and scimitars and genies, of mathematicians and astronomers and storytellers; a time when the gorgeous East held half the world in thrall. Unfortunately, like other golden ages in other climes it developed the seeds of its own destruction; indeed, the supreme epoch of Arab civilization was inaugurated with treachery and blood.

For it was not the Umayyad dynasty—conquerors of central Asia, North Africa, and Spain—that was to preside over the flowering of Arab culture, but a new dynasty, the Abbasids. These were descendants of Mohammed's uncle Abbas and like the Umayyads were proud members of the original Quraish tribe of Mecca. Thus when the Umayyad Caliph Waleed ibn Malik for some obscure personal reason insulted Ali ibn Abdulla Abbas, grandson of the Prophet's uncle, and had him flogged through the streets of Damascus in 710 he started one of those interclan feuds which could only be resolved in blood.

After ibn Abbas's public humiliation the Abbasid family withdrew from Damascus to live in the desert and there plot revenge. Mohammed, ibn Abbas's son, determined on nothing less than the complete overthrow of the Umayyad dynasty. To this end he patiently organized a widespread underground propaganda campaign, sending "missionaries" throughout the Arab world. These Abbasid agents whispered that the Umayyads, sunk in luxury and sin, no longer followed the precepts of Islam and had become mere despots. They also whispered (falsely) that the Abbasids had inherited the mantle of Ali, the Prophet's son-in-law, thus winning the support of numerous Shias to whom Ali's memory was still sacred. The Abbasid propaganda, which was carried on for decades, was in fact most successful in the East, in central Asia and Persia where the Shia sect was powerful.

While the Abbasids thus waged their campaign of subversion, Umayyad caliphs came and went. The popular nicknames bestowed on some of these rulers indicate the general decline in Umayyad character: Yezeed the Foolish, Waleed the Libertine, Yezeed the Drunkard, and finally Merwan the Ass. The uprisings and civil wars attendant upon the struggle between Umayyads and Abbasids were too complex to be recounted here; suffice it to say that in 750 the Umayyads were decisively beaten at the battle of the Zab (a river in eastern Syria). Merwan the Ass, last of the Umayyad caliphs, escaped the defeat of his army only to be murdered shortly afterward by Abbasid agents in Egypt.

Abu al-Abbas became the first caliph of the new dynasty and soon earned the nickname *As Saffah*— Shedder of Blood. For it was on the orders of the new Abbasid caliph that all the members of the Umayyad family were invited to a banquet of peace and reconciliation. But before the meal was served, Abbasid soldiers fell upon the ninety unarmed Umayyads present and slaughtered them all. Other Umayyads were hunted down and slain throughout the Arab world— but from this wholesale vengeance one Umayyad escaped.

He was Abdul Rahman ibn Muawiya, an intrepid young man who fled first to the Berbers of North Africa, among whom he trained himself for five years in Berber methods of warfare and built up a small but devoted following. Then in 756 he crossed over to Spain, where he soon deposed the local governor and made himself ruler of the Arab kingdom al-Andalus. In 763 Abdul Rahman defeated an Abbasid army sent to oust him, and thereafter the Arab Empire was split in two—with Umayyads governing Spain while Abbasid caliphs ruled in the East.

Meanwhile, in 754 the Shedder of Blood had died and was succeeded by Abu Jafar Mansoor, who devoted the early years of his caliphate to the suppression of Shia rebellions and to pondering a problem he had inherited from his predecessor: to find a capital. For the Umayyads had ruled too long in Damascus for it to be a secure Abbasid stronghold. Having considered and rejected several alternative cities, Mansoor decided to build a new capital for Islam. He had surveys made throughout the Near East and finally settled on an area (in present-day Iraq) between the Tigris and Euphrates rivers where these important trade routes were only twenty miles apart. Thus the new city would command the commerce of India, Syria, Persia, and Arabia. In May 763 Caliph Mansoor set up his tents and commenced construction.

It is said that Mansoor designed the new capital

himself—its layout was certainly unusual. It was two miles in diameter and perfectly round; its mighty circular walls pierced by four gates. Just inside those walls an inner circle of government office buildings was constructed; then concentric rings of houses; and finally, in the very center of the city, the huge golden palace of the caliph. No expense was spared to make the City of Peace, as Mansoor named it, the most splendid in all the world. There were numerous palaces, rich mansions, and beautiful mosques. Broad boulevards radiated from the center, crossed by colorfully tiled streets. There were public gardens wherein sparkling fountains played, exotic markets, and graceful minarets (towers from which the faithful were called to prayer). Only in one respect was Mansoor's will thwarted—the city's inhabitants (who soon numbered hundreds of thousands) could not be brought to call it the City of Peace. They still used the old, traditional name of the village that had once occupied its site: Baghdad.

Baghdad reached the zenith of its glory under the caliphs Haroun al-Raschid (786–809) and his son, al-Mamun (813–833). Suburbs as glittering as the original round city of Mansoor stretched for miles around its walls. It was the trading center of West and East—Arab ships traded regularly with China, India, Malaya, the East Indies, and Africa south to Madagascar. Here the silks and spices of Asia, the jewels, gold, and artifacts of Cathay, reached the Western world. And under the genial rule of the early Abbasid caliphs Baghdad became also a center of art, learning, literature, and pleasure. It was, as Richard Burton pointed out, "a Paris of the ninth century." Something of the city's spirit is reflected in the exotic tales of *The Thousand and One Nights*—really a collection of stories from India, Persia, Egypt, Arabia, and all the Orient, in which Haroun al-Raschid himself is a character along with Aladdin, Sinbad the Sailor, Ali Baba, and Scheherazade, the concubine who must beguile her king with marvelous tales every night to preserve her life every morning.

But Baghdad was not the only center of Arab culture. The older cities of Damascus in Syria and Alexandria in Egypt and the new cities of Cairo and Tunis also prospered. And far to the west in Umayyad al-Andalus the Spanish cities of Cordova, Seville, Valencia, and Granada developed under Islam as famous centers of art and learning. There too were to be found beautiful palaces like the incomparable Alhambra in Granada, great irrigation projects, huge libraries, universities, and a truly cosmopolitan civilization. All of this flourishing, be it remembered, during those centuries when Western Europe was struggling through its Middle Ages, when Paris and London were little more than collections of stone and mud-thatched huts, when (with the brief exception of the reign of Charlemagne at the beginning of the ninth century) every local noble was to some extent a law unto himself, when life was short, savage, and brutish and only in Byzantium was the memory of an older, civilized West retained.

It would require a book at least as long as this one to recount in detail all the contributions to the world's culture that flowed from Islam during this period (roughly A.D. 800 to A.D. 1200). Mathematics, for example. Not only did the scholars of Islam devise the numerals we still call Arabic, they also probably discovered the concept of zero, made *al jubr* (algebra) an exact science, discovered the trigonometrical ratios of sine, cosine, tangent, and cotangent, and laid the foundations for analytical geometry. And Arab research in astronomy remained far in advance of European research until well into the sixteenth century.

The Arab love of poetry was extended into a love of learning in every field of literature, philosophy, and science. The Caliph al-Mamun organized hundreds of scholars to translate into Arabic the ancient works of Greece, Rome, Egypt, and Persia, and it was through these translations that much of the culture of the ancient world was eventually to be rediscovered in the West.

The first free public hospital known to history had been opened by Haroun al-Raschid and by Mamun's time Baghdad could offer several medical schools, where physicians and surgeons were appointed to lecture students. Doctors, druggists, and orthopedic surgeons were all licensed and supervised by the government. In 872 the idea of free public hospitals spread to Egypt, and soon thereafter such institutions were to be found everywhere in the Moslem world, from Spain to India. For nearly four centuries medicine was an almost exclusively Arabic science. When Western Christian kings fell ill they contrived, despite their hostility toward Islam, to procure the services of doctors trained at Arab universities.

Nor was all this learning the province of specialized scholars alone. Literacy was widespread; there was a library attached to every mosque. During the ninth century there were no fewer than one hundred bookshops in a single Baghdad suburb; at Cordova at about the same time there were no less than seventy libraries.

In architecture too the Arabs excelled. Of course they inherited many architectural styles from the older empires of Rome, Persia, and Egypt; but they combined elements of each to form a distinctive style of their own. Their mosques and palaces especially—in stone, brick, marble, or covered with glazed tiles—were huge and yet light, delicate, and airy. To this day the beauty of such buildings as the mosque called the Dome of the Rock in Jerusalem and the palace of the Alhambra in Granada is part of the world's heritage.

It was through Arab trade with the Orient, Western Europe, and (surprisingly) Russia and Scandinavia that agricultural techniques and products known previously only to Asia were eventually established in Africa and Europe. Orange trees were first brought from China to Islam and thence to North Africa and

Spain; sesame, carobs, maize, rice, lemons, melons, and apricots were all first cultivated in the Arab world before reaching Christendom. Furthermore, Arab agricultural techniques were very progressive; to this day the entire Spanish vocabulary on irrigation is derived from Arabic.

Because the Prophet's original enemies had been idolators, and perhaps also deriving from Jewish tradition, it was forbidden to Moslems to make any likeness of the human face or form either in painting or statuary. For this reason fine art in the world of Islam developed largely as the art of design. Its triumphs were to be seen not only in city planning and architecture, but also in the intricate stucco tracery decorating mosques and palaces, in the beautiful geometric designs of colorful tile work, and even in gorgeous gardens in which trees, shrubs, water, and flowers provided natural color and form for Arabic artists.

Now we have described all these cultural achievements, as indeed we have described the Moslem empire, as "Arabic." But what does this really mean? It has been estimated that during the reign of the Abbasids "Arabs" could only have comprised 2 or 3 percent of all Islam—the rest being Indians, Persians, Jews, Greeks, Egyptians, Berbers, Spaniards, and innumerable other nationalities and races. It has been suggested that since the "Arabs" had been mixing with subject populations for nearly two centuries by the time of Haroun al-Raschid perhaps the very word "Arab" had better be reserved for those Bedouin tribesmen who remained in the Arabian deserts. And therefore, it has been urged, it is incorrect to ascribe to the "Arabs" the cultural achievements of Islam.

Of course no one would deny that Islamic culture was cosmopolitan—that Christians and Jews figured prominently in medicine, that gardening was an ancient art of the Persians, that Islamic Spain was mostly the creation of the Berbers, that Egyptians contributed much to astronomy or Greeks to philosophy. But that is the whole point. Aside from the fact that many of the most prominent artists and thinkers of Islam were indeed Arabs, it must be remembered that Arabs or those proudly claiming Arab descent remained the absolute ruling class in the empire. That they permitted and even encouraged the cultural contributions of their subject peoples was in itself a mark of cultural genius. For example, at a time when Jews were being massacred and persecuted throughout Western Europe, in the Moslem world they were honored scholars, doctors, jurists, and even highly placed political advisors to the caliphs. While Christian monks in Europe were busily erasing ancient Greek and Latin manuscripts in order to use the paper for endless copies of the Testaments, Arabic scholars were preserving and translating these priceless texts. And over all the empire the Arabic language spread its international mantle without displacing local tongues.

To end this discussion it may be instructive to compare the results of Arab dominion with the aftermath of the twelfth-century Mongol conquests in the Near East. Like the Arabs, the Mongols when they burst out of Eastern Asia were illiterate, wandering tribesmen, and like the Arabs they were to conquer a huge empire. But where under Arab rule a splendid and flourishing civilization arose, when the Mongols conquered these same regions they created nothing but heaps of smoking ruins and pyramids of skulls—such were their monuments. And the same could be said for Huns, Vandals, Avars, and many of the other conquering mass migrations that destroyed everything in their paths. The Arabs, except in the heat of battle, did not destroy—they built; they did not massacre defeated peoples but rather integrated them into a new, more tolerant, pluralistic society. Nor did they, like the Goths, merely copy the culture of the conquered, but rather they developed it into higher forms. Many nations, many races, helped to build the splendid edifice of Islamic civilization—but the original architects of the whole inspiring structure were the Arabs.

If the splendor of the caliph's court in Baghdad was oriental, so too was the Abbasid system of government. It will be recalled that the early caliphs, ruling from Medina and then from Damascus, had been men of simple habits and an almost puritanically severe lifestyle. They ruled their vast dominions very loosely, through governors and generals, content to leave direct administration in the hands of local bureaucrats. During the rule of the later Umayyads the caliphs themselves began to take on the pomp and circumstance of kings while building up a more direct system of government with local officials increasingly appointed by and responsible to the caliphate. But with the advent of the Abbasids the successors to the Prophet of God became absolute despots, ruling like Roman emperors or Persian kings of kings. The bureaucracy of Islam was centered in Baghdad, and like bureaucracies before and since, it fed upon its own power until it had swollen to a vast and cumbersome size.

Aside from maintaining order throughout the empire, the prime duty and great problem of this government was the collection of taxes—taxes for financing the splendor of Baghdad, for paying the caliph's soldiery, for undertaking vast irrigation projects, building canals (several connected the Tigris and Euphrates rivers near Baghdad), and of course for paying the tax collectors. Now the early Arab conquerors had imposed taxes only upon non-Moslems; the faithful were free of obligation. But as more and more of the conquered adopted Islam, the number of taxable subjects within the empire steadily shrank. The solution adopted by the Umayyad caliphs was to tax Moslems as well as infidels. Furthermore, history teaches us that taxes never go down but always rise, and the taxes in Islam were no exception to this rule: they rose steadily as the expenditure of the top-heavy central government increased. Resentment over taxes had been a powerful factor in the overthrow of the Umayyads, but the Abbasids did not heed this lesson.

Under Haroun al-Raschid the problem of collecting taxes was aggravated by the establishment of rival dynasties in distant parts of the empire—the Umayyads in Spain and then in 800 the breakaway Berbers of North Africa, who paid only nominal tribute to Baghdad. Caliph Haroun resorted to a disastrous solution to this vexing problem: he farmed out tax collection to local governors and military commanders. These individuals did not fail to line their own pockets and became increasingly independent of the caliph's authority. Under the circumstances it should come as no surprise to learn that the Abbasid caliphs, even in their days of greatest glory, were constantly putting down rebellions.

One of the most serious of these uprisings was that led by one Babak (816–837) in central Asia. Babak preached the breakup of the great estates of the wealthy and a redistribution of land to the peasants. A guerrilla leader of great ability, he defeated four Abbasid armies and held out for some twenty years before he was finally crushed. Thirty years later there was another rebellion of a different kind—that of the Zanj or black slaves. Unlike ancient Egypt and Rome the Islamic empire did not rely primarily on slaves for manual labor; that kind of work was carried out by peasants and artisans, and slaves were mainly employed as household servants or soldiers. But there were exceptions. One of these was the huge project of draining the marshes of southern Iraq to reclaim the land for agriculture. Thousands of black slaves were imported from East Africa for this purpose, and in 869 they rose in revolt. At first they enjoyed considerable success; their rebellion spread into southern Persia, they captured the great port city of Basra and even for a while threatened Baghdad itself. Black troops of the caliph's army refused to fight the rebels and often went over to their side. Finally after fourteen years the Zanj were defeated. It may be well to point out here that Islam was relatively free from racial prejudice; certainly the Moslem world was less guilty of racial bigotry and hatred than Christendom. Although there were without doubt racial overtones to the Zanj rebellion, the Zanj were fighting primarily against slavery, not against racial persecution.

These uprisings shook the empire but did not seriously endanger it. Of much graver consequence was the empire-wide rebellion of the Ismailis. These were a branch of the Shias who took their name from Ismail, the seventh descendant of Ali, the Prophet's son-in-law. Denouncing the Abbasids as despots and usurpers, the Ismailis copied the Abbasid technique of sending out missionaries to conduct underground propaganda. These agents preached throughout the empire that Ismail's son Mohammed would soon return to earth as the Mahdi (Messiah) to lead the faithful back to the true precepts of Islam. On a more practical level they advocated greater equality and a redistribution of wealth. The rapidity of Ismaili success was a measure of popular discontent with the Baghdad caliphate. In 901 the Ismailis won over the governor of Yemen (formerly Saba) to their cause, and in 908 they installed their imam (leader), Ubaydallah, as the first caliph of a rival dynasty in Tunisia, calling itself the Fatimid dynasty after the Prophet's daughter Fatima, the wife of Ali. In 969 the Fatimids conquered Egypt and founded the city of Cairo, which with its al-Azhar university soon became one of the great intellectual and spiritual centers of Islam. During the next century the Ismaili creed spread into Palestine, Syria, Persia, and western Arabia, while a Fatimid fleet conquered Sicily from the Byzantines and even invaded southern Italy. Eventually the Ismailis were to break into several smaller sects, with millions of followers in India, Pakistan, Syria, and East Africa, the Imams of one of these sects becoming the Aga Khans of our own day.

Thus, while Arabic culture reached the zenith of its

brilliance under the Abbasids, the unity of Islam was
shattered. Spain, North Africa, Tunisia, Egypt—all
asserted their independence of Baghdad. Even at home
the Abbasid caliphs found their authority slipping from
their grasp. For the armies of the commander of the
faithful were no longer composed of the faithful. The
great hosts that various Abbasid rulers led unsuccessfully against Byzantium from time to time were no
longer hordes of fanatical Moslem volunteers shouting,
"Allahu akbar!" as they rode into battle. Beginning as
early as the reign of Haroun al-Raschid, Abbasid forces
were increasingly mercenaries recruited from among
the wild Turkish tribes of central Asia. These semi-
barbarians, barely converted to Islam, possessed those
rough, warlike fighting qualities that Arabs and Persians used to luxury had lost. Just as later Roman
emperors found themselves forced to seek martial virtues not among their own citizens but among the bar-
baric German tribes from beyond the Rhine, so the
Abbasid caliphs had to rely on the Turks. And just as
the German mercenaries soon grew too powerful to control, so too did the Turks.

These Turkish warriors were for the most part
slaves. Called Mamelukes (owned ones) by their Abbasid masters, they were specially trained warriors
who depended for their very lives upon the whim of the
caliph. But this dependence soon became a two-way
street. Step by step the Mamelukes encroached upon
the caliphate until by the middle of the ninth century
the Abbasid caliphs were virtually prisoners of their
own armies. Turkish Mamelukes made and deposed
caliphs at their will. The Fatimids in Egypt also employed Mamelukes, with the same result; they too were
eventually dominated by this foreign military caste.

Then in 1055 a Turkish tribe known as the Seljuks
burst out of central Asia, sweeping all before them (the
Mamelukes were loath to fight fellow Turks). Only recently converted to Islam, these semibarbaric warriors
conquered Persia, Iraq, and Syria. They also drove the

Byzantines from much of Asia Minor—something the Arabs had never been able to do. Seljuk leaders, adopting the title of sultan (ruler), took over the temporal reins of government, leaving the caliphs as mere spiritual figureheads. So although both Abbasid and Fatimid caliphs continued to maintain their titles, between the Mamelukes in Egypt and the Seljuks in the East real power in the Arab world (except for North Africa and Spain, where the Seljuks never penetrated) had passed into Turkish hands. There it was to remain until our own day.

And what of the original Arabs, those lords of the desert who had formed the vanguard of Islam and presided over its golden age? Almost all had long since become so submerged into the cosmopolitan empire that they were indistinguishable from their neighbors. As for those Bedouin desert tribesmen who had refused to be so absorbed, they maintained their precious but poverty-stricken independence in Arabia itself. About them the Arab historian Ibn Khaldoun observed, "Every Arab regards himself as worthy to rule, and it is rare to find one of them submitting willingly to another."

The minarets and golden domes, the fabled cities and universities, the libraries, hospitals, and mosques, the glittering pageantry, the glamor and the poetry of Islam's golden age, were to endure yet a little while longer. But with the ascendancy of the Turks Arabic civilization began its long, slow decline. Writing from the perspective of the fourteenth century, Ibn Khaldoun sadly reflected on the past splendor of the Arabic empire: "And God inherits the earth and its inhabitants and he is the best heir of all."

But there were and are other inheritors of the golden age of Arabic civilization. For many Christian scholars came to study at the splendid universities in al-Andalus and Sicily, later returning to their own nations to pass on what they had learned of Arabic arts and sciences. And thousands of Jews who could still move freely between Moslem and Catholic lands spread Arabic knowledge of mathematics, astronomy, medicine, and agriculture throughout Christendom. Through these sources was transmitted not only the culture of Islam but also the cultures of ancient Greece and Rome, preserved by Moslem scholars and about to revitalize a Europe emerging from its Dark Ages. So we are all of us in some sense the heirs of Islam.

CHAPTER FIVE

The Sign of the Cross

In the Name of God, the Compassionate, the Merciful
But others have come in their place after them: they
have made an end of prayer, and have gone after their
own lusts; and in the end they shall meet with evil.

KORAN, XIX

For nearly four hundred years after the death of the
Prophet, Islam—led in turn by Arab and Persian caliphs, then by Seljuk sultans—had been everywhere on
the offensive. Despite internal dissensions and civil
wars the dominions of the faithful had steadily grown.
The *muezzin*'s call to prayers was heard in golden Bok-
hara and Samarkand, in the jeweled cities of India, in
the capitals of the black kingdoms of central Africa, in
Cordova and Seville, and at the gates of Byzantium.
But now around the year 1000 the flow of conquest
began to ebb. Like the shifting of a tide at night, this
ebb was, at first, imperceptible.

It began in the West, where for four centuries Christendom had cowered before the might of the Moslems.
Not only all of formerly Christian North Africa but
also Sicily and Spain had fallen; Islamic armies had
penetrated southern France and Italy—and no man
could say how much longer Byzantium would hold out

against the faithful. It mattered little to Europeans that Islam was now divided into Umayyad, Fatimid, and Seljuk domains; the Moslem world was seen as monolithic and its threat as imminent. In this respect Europeans of the eleventh century regarded Islam with much the same uninformed dread as Americans of the twentieth century were to view communism, another religiously fervent, supranational ideology backed by awesome material might.

To seek the beginnings of Christian resurgence we must turn to Spain, where the first Arab conquerors had committed one small but grievous error: They had allowed a remnant of the defeated infidels to find sanctuary in the mountainous northwest corner of the peninsula. There in those craggy strongholds the Christian refugees had slowly, painfully built up a state. This was the Kingdom of Leon, which in the two hundred years following its establishment gradually extended its territory and power until during the tenth century it felt strong enough to counterattack the Umayyad rulers of al-Andalus. Thus commenced five hundred years of almost constant warfare known to Spaniards as La Reconquista (the Reconquest)—a seemingly endless struggle that developed in the Spanish temper those characteristics of bravery, morbidity, black humor, and intolerance for which it has ever since been famous.

The Reconquista was much too complex to recount in detail: Christians fought Moslems, Christians fought Christians, Moslems fought Moslems, both sides made alliances irrespective of religious faith, and it was sometimes impossible to tell which side anyone was really on. To further complicate matters, as the power of the Umayyad dynasty decayed, semi-independent Moslem principalities rose and vanished and rose again, while Christian kings—by following the ancient Gothic practice of dividing their domains among *all* their male heirs—fragmented northern Spain into such petty, quarrelsome states as Navarre, Aragon, Castile, nd others. The famous statesmen and warriors of hese ages of strife were many on both sides, but among hem two were outstanding: the Moslem vizier (prime ninister) Ibn abu Aamir, known as al-Mansur-billah Through God Victorious), and the Christian knight Rodrigo Diaz de Vivar, known as *El Mio Cid Campea-or* (My Lord Champion). They lived at different times, nd their careers reflect the changing pattern and na-ure of the long struggle for Spain.

Al-Mansur became vizier to the young Umayyad uler Hisham II in A.D. 976. Although born into poverty Mansur had already proven himself a young man of rilliant intellect and driving ambition. He had grad-ated with honors from Cordova University and quickly rorked his way up through the Umayyad civil service. Iis intelligence, tact, and total lack of scruples even-ually won him the top government post, and since Iisham II was a mere child in 976, the new vizier ruled l-Andalus pretty much as he pleased.

After ruthlessly suppressing a Moslem army rebel-ion, Mansur invaded Christian Leon in 981. The king f Leon had helped the rebels, and Mansur was deter-nined to teach that monarch (Ramiro III) a lesson. Ramiro's "education" was swift and harsh. After ut-erly routing the combined Christian forces of Leon, Iavarre, and Castile at Rueda, Mansur's army cap-ured Simancas; the town was looted and its inhabit-nts massacred. Then the Moslem forces marched on o the city of Leon itself, which they besieged. Although he onset of winter compelled the Moslems to retire, he Kingdom of Leon had been reduced to little more han a satellite of al-Andalus.

Four years later (in 985) Mansur again marched orth, this time against the great port city of Barce-ona. This Christian stronghold had long held itself loof from the endless wars of Spain. Nonetheless, rhen Mansur's army took Barcelona by storm on July , 985, the city was pillaged and burned while its cit-zens were either massacred or carried off into slavery.

The Christian Counterattack

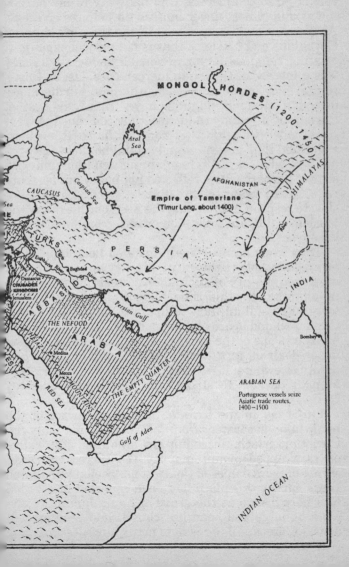

MONGOL HORDES (1200–1450)

Aral Sea

CAUCASUS

Caspian Sea

AFGHANISTAN

HIMALAYAS

Empire of Tamerlane
(Timur Leng, about 1400)

TURKS

Tigris

Euphrates River

Baghdad

Tigris River

P E R S I A

Indus River

INDIA

Damascus

CRUSADER
KINGDOMS

Jerusalem

Persian Gulf

Bombay

ABBASID

THE NEFOOD

A R A B I A

HEJAZ

RED SEA

Medina

Mecca

MOUNTAINS

THE EMPTY QUARTER

ARABIAN SEA

Portuguese vessels seize
Asiatic trade routes,
1400–1500

Gulf of Aden

INDIAN OCEAN

Mansur's savagery at Simancas and Barcelona stands in startling contrast to the enlightened policies of the earlier Arab conquerors, who had very rarely burned towns and almost never massacred helpless civilians. An element of ferocity was entering the wars between Christians and Moslems that is not easy to explain. It was not religious fervor, for much of Mansur's army was composed of Christian mercenaries, just as Christian armies included Moslem warriors. Furthermore, although Moslems might behave frightfully against Christians in enemy countries, they continued to treat Christians with perfect tolerance at home. It has been suggested that Mansur simply could not abide any opposition whatsoever to his flaming ambition and will, so that his barbarities reflected not policy but personal rage. In any event the great vizier's enemies were not slow to respond in kind, and the wars of Christians and Moslems in Spain grew fiercer and more fanatical as time went on.

Thus when Mansur again invaded Leon in 988, his army laid waste to the entire country and deliberately destroyed the city of Leon after massacring most of its inhabitants. By this time Mansur had waged some forty successful military campaigns against the Christian north and against Moslem rebels at home. Al-Andalus was one of the great powers of the world, and its vizier dealt on terms of equality with kings and emperors elsewhere. It was at this apogee of his glory that Mansur decided to strike one final blow to destroy Christian Spain.

Far away in the extreme northwest corner of the peninsula, separated from al-Andalus not only by Christian principalities but also by range after range of snowcapped mountains, lay the sacred Christian shrine of Saint James of Compostela. Some two hundred years earlier this place had been revealed in a vision to a holy bishop as the grave of Saint James the disciple. A large and beautiful church had been erected over the site, and as a result of many miracles occurring there Santiago de Compostela (Santiago is Spanish for Saint James) had become one of the greatest centers of pilgrimage in Europe. "It is to the Christians what the Kaaba of Mecca is to the Moslems," observed one of Mansur's advisors. So although Santiago de Compostela was not a military target of any value, its capture would be a moral and spiritual triumph for Islam.

Sending part of his army by sea, Mansur led the rest across those fearsome mountains. When both forces met outside Santiago de Compostela on August 11, 997, they found the town deserted. One solitary old monk was praying at the tomb of Saint James. "What are you doing here?" demanded Mansur. "I am praying," the old man replied simply. "You may go on praying," said the great vizier. Mansur ordered a guard placed over the tomb to protect the monk and to prevent its desecration. Then both the church and the town of Compostela were completely obliterated—not one stone was left standing upon another. After a week of ravaging the countryside the Moslem army withdrew, carrying off the great bells of the church to serve as lamps in the principal mosque of Cordova.

In August 1002, a few years after his return from Compostela, al-Mansur died. His memory was revered among Moslems for his many military victories, but in Christian Spain his Latinized name, Almanzor, became a symbol of hatred and fear ever after.

Soon after al-Mansur's death civil war broke out over who should wield the great power he had centralized in Cordova. Various sections of the army, Berbers, European mercenaries, and "Arabs" advanced the claims of various candidates for the Umayyad throne. Battles and assassinations followed until in 1031 the entire edifice of Umayyad power came crumbling down. Al-Andalus disintegrated, and such cities as Cordova and Seville, Valencia and Granada, Saragossa and Toledo became independent principalities. Thirty years of warfare between these small states then ensued. Fortunately for the Moslems, at that time the Christians were also engaged in civil wars. Ferdinand I of Navarre, having conquered Leon and Castile in 1037, had thereupon proclaimed himself "emperor of all Spain." He was in fact the single most powerful monarch ruling in that much-divided land.

The second of our warriors—Rodrigo Diaz de Vivar *El Mio Cid Campeador*—was born in 1043 (some four decades after Mansur's death) in the town of Vivar in Christian Castile. Rodrigo's father, though poor, was of the lesser Castilian nobility, and his son was raised a warrior. At an early age Rodrigo was sent to learn the martial arts of knighthood at the court of Emperor Ferdinand I.

Like all good heroes of medieval chivalry Rodrigo devoted his youth to single-combat victories over local tyrants and to acts of Christian charity—once he helped a ragged leper on the road to Leon. The leper turned out to be none other than Saint Lazarus in disguise; in a vision he promised Rodrigo that his charity would be rewarded by a great victory to be granted him after his death. When Ferdinand I died in 1065, his "empire" was divided among his heirs. Rodrigo became commander-in-chief of the army of one of these heirs Sancho the Strong, King of Castile. Sancho determined to reunite his father's domains by conquering the inheritance of his brother, Alfonso, King of Leon. But the crafty Alfonso struck first; he had Sancho murdered and then assumed the title of Alfonso VI, King of Leon *and* Castile. Of course Rodrigo, as Sancho's ex-henchman, found neither favor nor employment with the new king. After a series of intrigues against him Rodrigo was finally banished from Castile and Leon in 1079.

Accomplished by some three hundred knights, Rodrigo hired himself out as a soldier of fortune to various petty Moslem rulers in the south. An example of how intermixed Christian and Islamic cultures were is to be found in the title Rodrigo now gained: *El Mio Cid Campeador*. All the words in that phrase are Spanish

except the word *Cid*. That is a mispronunciation of the
Arabic *sayiid* or lord.

Having made himself undisputed master of the
north, Alfonso VI now decided that the time had come
to drive the Moslems entirely from the peninsula. To
this end he began a campaign of conquest against the
divided remains of al-Andalus, and by 1085 he had
carried the Christian banners to within three miles of
Granada and final victory. But this offensive was to
prove the undoing of that rash king who made war
without the help of El Cid.

For in their utter desperation the Moslems took the
utterly desperate step of seeking help from their brethren in North Africa. Since 1050 North Africa had been
in the hands of a sect of Moslem fanatics known as al-
Murabitin (the Holy Ones), an army of wild Saharan
desert nomads who made even the fierce Berbers seem
peaceful. The al-Murabitin were the zealous puritans
of Islam, only semicivilized and as foreign to the cul-
tured Moslems of Spain as they were to the Christian
world. If they crossed the straits to help Granada, there
was little doubt they would remain to rule. But as
Mutamid ibn Abbad, Moslem King of Seville, remarked, "[I] would rather be a camel driver in Africa
than a swineherd in Castile." The dangerous invitation
was therefore extended to Yusuf ibn Tashfin, emperor
of the al-Murabitin, or as their mispronounced name
has entered Western history, the Almoravides.

Ibn Tashfin crossed over to Spain with a mighty
army and met the forces of King Alfonso at the battle
of Sagrajas on October 23, 1086. The Moslem victory
was total—Alfonso's army was completely destroyed,
and he barely escaped with his life and a handful of
followers. All of Christian Spain believed that had El
Cid been fighting for Alfonso the outcome would have
been different. Accordingly, the chastised king invited
El Cid back from exile in the spring of 1087. Meanwhile, to the surprise and relief of the Spanish Moslems, ibn Tashfin had returned to Africa with most of

his army, leaving behind only three thousand of his terrible Holy Ones to help the King of Seville.

Perhaps because of this the pride of Alfonso began to swell again. In 1089 he again decreed the banishment of El Cid, and that doughty champion made himself master of the Moslem city of Valencia. In various campaigns he defeated Moslem princes, the King of Aragon (a Christian), and the Count of Barcelona. But while El Cid was making his name feared along the Spanish Mediterranean coast, King Alfonso had resumed his attack on al-Andalus. Once again the Moslems appealed to the Holy Ones for aid, and once again Emperor ibn Tashfin led an army into Spain. But this time the Almoravides had come to stay. Easily brushing aside Alfonso's forces, the Holy Ones methodically conquered all of the small Moslem states of al-Andalus—with the sole exception of Valencia, where they were beaten back by El Cid.

But on July 10, 1099, the great Christian *Campeador* died peacefully in his bed. Since he alone had been able to hold Valencia against the Almoravides, it now seemed certain that the city would fall. But how were the Christians within the walls (and Moslems too, for that matter) to break through the besieging Almoravide host and escape? For it was well known that the Holy Ones took no prisoners when they captured a city. According to legend El Cid's wife devised the scheme of strapping his fully armored dead body to his horse and sallying from the walls of Valencia led by this apparition. When the Holy Ones saw the Valencians charging upon them led by a man presumably resurrected from the dead, they fled in superstitious terror. The Valencians made good their escape, and as Saint Lazarus had foretold, Rodrigo Diaz de Vivar had won a victory after his death. Valencia of course was abandoned to the Holy Ones.

So far the legend. The truth was more mundane. El Cid's wife defended Valencia for three years after his death and *then* fled the city, carrying her husband's corpse with her. But legend was much more important than truth anyhow. For El Cid, like the knights of the Round Table, became the very model of the ideal Christian warrior, his name and legend a great force in the long agony of the Reconquista—which now, with the advent of the Almoravides, was to be delayed for another four centuries.

But while the battle for Spain thus surged back and forth between Christians and Moslems, great events were taking place in the East. There in the year 1071 the Byzantine army (including many contingents of English, Norman, and French troops) was completely defeated by the Seljuk Turks at the battle of Malazkirt in eastern Asia Minor. So terrible was the Christian rout that it seemed nothing could now prevent the Seljuks from capturing Byzantium itself and then overrunning all of Christendom from the east. This probably would have occurred had not Alp Arslan, the Seljuk emperor, decided to subdue rebellious provinces in central Asia instead. So Byzantium was granted yet another respite, though the Seljuks overran all of Asia Minor. But how long the great city on the Bosphorus would continue to shield Europe was a grim question.

Meanwhile the endless civil wars of Islam—between Fatimids, Abbasids, Seljuks, Shias, and Ismailis—had laid waste to much of the Near East. Palestine was especially hard hit by the passage of rival armies, and throughout the entire region law and security had vanished. For example, the most feared authority between Cairo and Baghdad was neither Fatimid nor Seljuk, but rather a branch of the Ismaili sect known as the Hashashin (eaters of hashish, a potent form of marijuana). Originating in Persia, this fanatical secret society waged an endless campaign of terror against all established government. Hashashin agents, presumably "high" on their dope, murdered generals, officials, caliphs, and sultans with deadly efficiency. Their very name, mispronounced by Christians, entered Western languages as the terrifying word "assassin." Secure in their strongholds hidden in the high hills of Syria (their leader was known as the Old Man of the Mountains), the Assassins kept Islam in fear for more than a century. Needless to say, between armies, Assassins, and brigands, the fate of Christians—both those who lived in the Near East and Europeans on pilgrimage to Jerusalem—was dire indeed.

All of which was much on the mind of Pope Urban II as he slowly made his way from Rome to attend a church council at the town of Clermont in France in the year 1095. News of Christian suffering in the East had moved His Holiness, as had warnings and appeals for help from Byzantium. Accordingly on November 27, 1095 Pope Urban, who was a noted orator, made the greatest speech of his life. He appealed not only to the assembled clerics at Clermont but to all the kings and lords of Christendom that they immediately march to the relief and rescue of their brethren in the East. They were to save Byzantium and to wrest control of the Holy Land from Islam. God would surely bless their mission, and by virtue of the holiness of their purpose they would wear the sign of the cross upon their tunics. Thus was ignited the passion of the first Crusade.

The cry of *Deus le vult* (God wills it) soon spread throughout Europe as once the cry of *Allahu akbar* had swept through Arabia. The great feudal nobles—moved by sincere religious convictions, greedy for the loot of the Orient, eager to establish kingdoms for themselves in the East, or simply lured by the smell of battle and adventure—gathered their private armies and prepared to march. But before they were fully organized, another kind of Crusade was launched. This was the so-called People's Crusade led by Peter the Hermit, a fanatical, uninformed monk, and one Walter-without-Belongings, an eager but impecunious knight. More than twenty thousand unarmed men, women, and children followed these leaders to death, disaster, and slavery on the plains of Asia Minor in the year 1096. The Byzantine Emperor Alexius, appalled by this formless mob, could do nothing to help them; the Seljuks, taking pity on some of the children, spared the youngest.

Meanwhile the real, armed Crusade made ready. It was led by Godfrey de Bouillon, Duke of Lotharingia (modern Belgium); Bohemonde the Norman, son of the Duke of Apulia (in Italy); Raymond de Saint Gilles, Count of Toulouse and ruler of much of southern France; and Robert, Duke of Normandy, eldest son of that William the Conqueror who in 1066 had invaded and subdued England to the Norman yoke. These were real, professional, able generals—and they led well-equipped, well-trained professional armies numbering, all told, some 150,000 men, of whom perhaps 20,000 were heavily armored knights. This was the first unified Christian counteroffensive against the Moslems; Islam was about to receive a deadly thunderbolt.

The Crusaders passed through Byzantium and with the help of the Emperor Alexius established a secure beachhead in Asia Minor. Thence they marched against the Seljuks, whom they easily defeated near Nicaea in June 1097. Accustomed to doing battle against the easy-going Byzantines, the Seljuks were completely unprepared for the savage enthusiasm of the Franks and Normans—indeed the very word Frank, used indiscriminately to describe all Crusaders, was soon to become a name of terror to Moslems everywhere. The Crusaders marched across Asia Minor, defeating Seljuk forces wherever they encountered them, and finally made their way through the Cilician Gates to conquer the great northern Syrian city of Antioch in October 1097. There as a reward for their zeal they discovered the remains of the very lance with which a Roman centurion had pierced Christ's body during the Crucifixion. Thus commenced that long commerce in bits of the "true lance," the "true cross," the "true shroud," the "true chalice," and other holy relics of the passion of Jesus with which Near Eastern merchants enriched European cathedrals and lined their own pockets, a commerce that has continued to our own day.

While the leaders of the Crusade argued about the division of spoils from Antioch and other captured territories, the Moslems of Syria were engaged in one of their endless civil wars—punctuated this time by the arrival of a Fatimid army from Egypt, which captured Jerusalem in the autumn of 1098. Perhaps reminded of their original purpose by this event, the Crusaders again marched south. Carrying all before them, the Christian host, led by Raymond de Saint Gilles and Godfrey de Bouillon, laid siege to Jerusalem on June 7, 1099. A few weeks later, on July 15, the Holy City fell. The rejoicing Crusaders made their way to the Holy Sepulchre of Christ through a sea of blood, massacring Egyptian soldiers, Moslem and Jewish civilians, and anyone else unlucky enough to witness their triumph. Five days earlier, far to the west, El Cid had died in Valencia.

Some of the Crusaders now established principalities for themselves out of their newly conquered domains. Bohemonde styled himself Prince of Antioch, Godfrey became Defender of the Holy Sepulchre in Jerusalem, Tancred (a nephew of Bohemonde) assumed the title Prince of Galilee. Many of the other leaders as well as much of the army returned to Europe, where for their services both their sins and their debts had been forgiven them by the Pope.

During the following decades the tiny Crusader states in Palestine gradually expanded into a feudal "Kingdom of Jerusalem" that controlled most of the Mediterranean coast from Antioch to Jaffa. But the thin boundaries of this Western bridgehead in Asia were never long secure, and the rivalries of its various feudal lords kept internal affairs in a constant uproar. Dependent on a precarious sea lifeline for supplies and reinforcements, the Kingdom of Jerusalem really relied on continuing dissensions within Islam for its continued existence. When the civil wars that wracked the Moslem world ended, so too would the Crusader states. Even with the Saracens divided (the name Saracen was bestowed on all Moslems, be they Abbasid, Fatimid, or Seljuk, by the Crusaders) the Frankish Kings of Jerusalem were constantly beseeching the West for help. Thus in the year 1144 a second Crusade, preached by Saint Bernard of Clairvaux and led by Louis VII of France and Conrad III of Germany, set out for the Holy Land. Poorly commanded and ill equipped, it never reached its destination; it was decimated by the Seljuks as it trudged across Asia Minor.

Some twenty years after the debacle of the second Crusade, the Seljuk Sultan Nureddin captured Damascus, brought Syria under control, and established a unified Moslem state to confront the Europeans in the Near East. Nureddin could deploy the resources not only of Syria but also of Iraq—and he had a secret agent planted within the rival Fatimid state of Egypt. This agent was named Salah al-Din, an extremely cunning and sophisticated warrior-politician better known to the West as Saladin the Great. Saladin rose to become vizier to the Fatimid ruler in Cairo; and when that ruler died in 1171, Saladin had amassed sufficient power to simply proclaim the end of the Fatimid caliphate and make himself sultan of Egypt. Three years later Nureddin died and Saladin also became sultan of Syria. He then turned his attention to the European intruders in Palestine, and by the year 1187 he had captured Jerusalem and thrown the infidels back onto a tiny strip of land along the Syrian coast. The Holy Land was once again in the hands of Islam.

When news of this disaster reached the West, a third Crusade was immediately proclaimed. This was to be the most ambitious and famous of all the Crusades. It was led by Philip Augustus of France, Frederick Barbarossa of Germany, and Richard the Lion-Hearted of England. Commanding formidable armies, these three mighty monarchs set out for the Holy Land by sea. Unfortunately Barbarossa was drowned en route, Philip Augustus had little real interest in crusading, and Richard, though a notable warrior, was a wretched politician. By the time the Crusaders reached Palestine in 1190, the English king had succeeded in alienating all the other leaders. The Germans soon went home and the French fought halfheartedly. Richard and his English won a few minor battles and recaptured a handful of Syrian port cities. But in the end Lion Heart had to be satisfied with a treaty whereby the wily Saladin did no more than grant Christian pilgrims the right to visit the holy shrines of Jerusalem. When Richard tried to make his way home to England, he was captured and held for ransom by the German Emperor Henry VI—an adventure that indicates the decline of genuine religious zeal in the crusading movement.

Perhaps the most successful of all later Crusades was the fourth—directed not against the Moslem world but rather against Byzantium. Pope Innocent III, who preached the Crusade, had not intended this misdirection. But Enrico Dandolo, the aged and cunning doge of Venice who provided both the fleet and the money to finance the expedition, insisted that the Crusaders dispose of the Byzantines (who, it was claimed, were in secret league with the Saracens) and thereby secure for Venice undisputed commercial sway over the eastern Mediterranean. Byzantium, which had withstood the fury of Moslem attack for five centuries, fell to the fourth Crusade in 1204. The Venetians and French knights pillaged the city thoroughly and then set up a Latin kingdom of Constantinople, which lasted for sixty years before being reclaimed by the Greeks. The fourth Crusaders never came anywhere near the Holy Land—they succeeded only in weakening the West's greatest bastion against Islam.

There was a fifth Crusade, which came near to conquering Egypt but ultimately failed, and a sixth Crusade which recaptured Jerusalem in 1229 but lost the city again in 1244. A seventh and an eighth Crusade, both led by the saintly Louis IX of France, proved futile (Louis died in Tunisia in 1270); and by the year 1300 the last Crusader strongholds in the Near East had been recaptured by the Moslems. The Holy Land was to remain part of Islam until the twentieth century.

When at last the Christian tide ebbed from the Near East, it left little behind of a positive nature. There were to be sure the Syrian-Palestinian coastal trading colonies established by the Crusaders, which were permitted to remain by Moslem authorities. For as Saladin wrote to the caliph of Baghdad in 1183, "The Venetians, the Genoese, and the Pisans bring into Egypt choice products of the West, especially arms and war materials. This constitutes an advantage for Islam and an injury for Christianity." But trade between Asia and Europe did not originate with the Crusades or end with them; the Christian presence in Palestine did little to either constrict or expand this commerce.

On the other hand the Christian invasions did make one lasting impression: the brutal treatment meted out to Moslems by Crusaders during their occupation of the Holy Land did much to permanently undermine Islam's traditional tolerance of other religions. Three centuries of intimate contact with Christian warriors in the Near East left a residue of disgust and resentment among Moslems that has not yet been eradicated.

The Crusades had a much greater effect on Europe than on Islam. For the religious fanaticism associated with them was turned against Jews, heretics, and political enemies of the Papacy. Each Crusade signaled the massacre of these unfortunates in the lands through which it passed; later Crusades were initiated not against Moslems but against, for example, the Albigensian heretics of southern France. The hatreds, bigotries, and civil strife to which the Crusades gave birth in Europe inflicted wounds upon European culture from which it took centuries to recover.

While the last Crusaders were still struggling to maintain themselves on the shores of the eastern Mediterranean, a far greater threat to Islam was developing in central Asia. There the great warrior Genghis Khan had succeeded in uniting the fierce pagan Mongolian nomadic tribes and welding them into a mighty army. In the years 1219–1225 he advanced through Turkestan into Persia and Afghanistan and westward into the Caucasus and southern Russia. In 1258 Hulagu Khan, grandson of the dreaded Genghis, advanced through Persia (utterly exterminating the Hashashin along the way) and into Asia Minor and Iraq, where he captured Baghdad. In the following year Hulagu's warriors struck west into Syria and captured Damascus, reaching the shores of the Mediterranean and the gates of Egypt by 1260.

Now we have spoken of this Mongol invasion as if it were like those previous incursions whereby Berbers or Seljuks had extended their sway over parts of Islam. But the Mongol advance was very different. When, for example, Hulagu took Baghdad in 1258, his army massacred all six hundred thousand of the city's inhabitants and kicked Mustasim, the last Abbasid caliph, to death before Hulagu's gloating eyes. The Mongols were uninterested in religion—they remained pagans and had no use for any of the works of civilization. Untold millions of people perished at their hands in holocausts that were not to be duplicated until our own more enlightened times. Wherever they passed—in the Near East, in central Asia, in Russia, in India, in China—they left behind them mountains of dead and the dust of great cities. They created deserts out of fruitful lands, deserts that remain today as their only monument. Not merely armies, not merely cities, not merely nations, but entire human cultures, were wiped out by the Mongol hordes. They struck a blow against Islam in the Near East from which it was never really to recover; compared to their invasion the Crusades were a mere pinprick.

And this was the terrible threat that in 1260 was poised to overwhelm Egypt and then perhaps all of North Africa. After the death of Saladin in 1193 his Egyptian-Syrian sultanate had disintegrated; and in 1250 Aybak, the Mameluke commander of the Egyptian army, seized the throne to become the first in a long line of Mameluke sultans. His successor, Qutuz, gathered a Mameluke army together in Syria, and in a battle of sheer desperation won a surprise victory over Hulagu's forces at Ain Jalut in Palestine on September 3, 1260. Qutuz's reward for this victory was to be murdered by one of his Mameluke officers named Baybars, who thereupon assumed the sultanate.

It will be recalled that for centuries the Mamelukes (almost all of whom were Turks) had formed a unique military-slave aristocracy in Egypt. Baybars, like other Mamelukes, had been captured and enslaved as a child (he was a Qipchaq Turk from the northern shores of the Caspian Sea), then raised in the Spartan military tradition for which Mamelukes had long been famous. Like Saladin he was sophisticated, cunning, and ruthless. He united Syria and Egypt under his rule, drove back the invading Mongols, and, almost incidentally, mopped up the last Crusader strongholds in the Near East. One of his cleverest moves was to set up a refugee Abbasid from Baghdad as a puppet caliph in Cairo, thereby lending an aura of respectability to his usurpation of the sultanate.

The line of Mameluke sultans was to last three hundred years. One of the secrets of its strength was the fact that it was not hereditary. Each Mameluke sultan imported his own slave-child successor who was then educated in Egypt and specifically trained for command. This system guaranteed a continuation of ability in the Mameluke line rather than the usual slow degeneration of a ruling family. Mameluke civilization in Egypt and Syria has been characterized as "brilliant," "cruel," "luxurious"—it was all of these and more: it was also strong, and to its strength the West owed in great measure its preservation from the Mongol holocaust.

Not that the Mongols were destroyed by Baybars; they remained in control of Persia and Mesopotamia for many years. In India they founded a dynasty known as the Moguls that lasted until the coming of the British Raj. And hordes of those fierce Asiatic nomads reappeared in Syria itself in the year 1400. This time they were led by another world-conquering military genius named Timur Leng (Timur the Lame or, in English, Tamerlane). After devastating Russia and India, Tamerlane turned west toward the Mediterranean, pillaged Aleppo and Damascus, massacred tens of thousands of people, and carried off into Asiatic slavery all the skilled artisans he could find. His armies did not press on into Egypt, however, but returned to Asia, where Tamerlane died soon after. Yet this bloody expedition struck hard at the roots of Mameluke power, as we shall see.

While Islam in the East was expelling the crusaders and fighting off Mongol invasions, far to the West it was steadily losing its grip on Spain. We left that wartorn peninsula in 1099, with El Cid dead, the Christian armies of Alfonso VI defeated, and the pleasant land of al-Andalus in the hands of the fierce Almoravides. The Holy Ones had built up an empire that stretched from the gates of Barcelona to the central African black kingdom of Ghana, from Morocco to the Libyan desert. But after the death of their Emperor ibn Tashfin the Almoravides could not hold their vast domain in Africa, while in al-Andalus they soon sank into the soft, luxurious life of Moslem Spain. During the twelfth century a new, fanatically fervent religious movement originating in the Saharan wastes replaced the decaying Almoravide power in al-Andalus. These were the al-Muwahhidin (Unifiers, mispronounced in Spanish as Almohades)—a fiercely puritanical sect who imposed unity upon Moslems with the sword and renewed the martial vigor of Islamic Spain. For many years they stiffened resistance to the Christian advance from the north before they too succumbed to the pleasures of life in al-Andalus.

After Alfonso VI that Christian advance was a slow, prolonged struggle. Defeats seemed always to balance victories, and as always the central problem of Christian disunity remained a plague. The various kingdoms of Leon, Navarre, Aragon, and Castile waxed and waned in strength but continued to jealously guard their independence at no matter what cost to the Reconquista.

It was with the advent of Almohade power in the peninsula that the nature of the Reconquista underwent a profound and ultimately disastrous change. For the fanatical Almohades undertook to "purify" the Moslem domains in al-Andalus. They harshly persecuted their Christian and Jewish subjects, expelling many, killing many, and converting others by the sword. In the process they destroyed that pluralistic society which had once been the glory of Islamic Spain. Until that time Moslems and Christians had been so intermixed, both culturally and racially, that the wars between them had seldom been total. But the rise of Moslem bigotry was matched by the growth of Christian intolerance, partly as a reaction to Almohade fanaticism, partly as a result of the increase in papal authority throughout Western Europe. During the last centuries of the Reconquista the fighting in Spain took on the bitter, hateful quality of what Moslems called *jihad* and Christians called Holy War.

Like the Christians of the north the Moslems of al-Andalus were plagued by dissensions as Almohade power decayed. A much more serious weakness was the Moslem dependence upon Africa as a source of reinforcement. Like the Almoravides before them, the Almohades ruled al-Andalus as only a part of their (principally) African empire. When that empire fell to pieces amid savage civil wars during the fourteenth century, the base of Moslem power in Spain was destroyed. Cut off from any effective help from Africa, Islamic Spain was forced into a steady retreat before a Christian power that could be easily reinforced at need from beyond the Pyrenees. Slowly the fabled land of al-Andalus shrank to the tiny proportions of the kingdom of Granada, the last Moslem foothold in Spain.

Then, toward the close of the fifteenth century, Christian Spain was finally united by the marriage of King Ferdinand of Leon and Aragon with Queen Isabella of Castile. Thereafter Christian power in the peninsula was overwhelming. The end of the seven-century struggle came in April 1492, when on the field of Santa Fe outside the walls of fallen Granada the "Catholic Monarchs" (as Ferdinand and Isabella are known to Spanish history) accepted the surrender of Boabdil, the last Moslem king. It is said that later, when Boabdil was riding off to exile in Africa, the unfortunate king paused atop the Mountain of the Sun to gaze back over his lost, golden domains and sighed in heartbreak. His mother spurred her horse close to her son's and said, "You do well to weep like a woman over what you could not defend like a man!" To this reproach Boabdil made no reply. But his sigh of regret, *la ultima suspira del Moro*, can be heard to this very day when the evening breeze caresses the hills beyond Granada.

CHAPTER SIX

Foreign Masters

In the Name of God, the Compassionate, the Merciful
The infidels lend one another mutual help. Unless ye
do the same, there will be discord in the land
and great corruption.

KORAN, VIII

While the Catholic Monarchs celebrated their entrance
into Boabdil's enchanting city with solemn masses and
Te Deums, the rejoicing of Europe beyond the Pyrenees
was to say the least restrained. For barely forty years
before the fall of Granada, Islam had made a conquest
in the East compared to which the Christian triumph
in Spain paled into insignificance. Oddly enough, the
chain of events that culminated in this great Moslem
victory originated with the terrible Mongol invasions
of the Near East.

The first of these, Hulagu Khan's murderous incur-
sion in 1258, had not only destroyed the Abbasid caliphate of Baghdad, it had also wrecked the Seljuk sultanate in Asia Minor. But after the Mongols had
passed, a young Turkish mercenary named Othman
gathered some of the shattered Seljuk forces together
and began to impose order amid the ruins. Only recently converted to Islam and speaking no Arabic, Oth-

man slowly extended his martial law through Asia Minor. After many years of struggle he created the only kind of state feasible amid the wreckage left by the Mongols—a military dictatorship of which he became the first sultan. His descendants during the following century continued his work of unification and rebuilding until they had brought almost all of Asia Minor, from the borders of the Byzantine Empire in the West to Persia in the East, under their sway. The original military dictatorship gradually developed a civilian structure of government and was called the Ottoman Empire after the tribe of its founder. The sultans and highest military commanders continued to be Turkish, speaking little Arabic and dispensing with the establishment of a religious caliphate (though they were devout Moslems). And the hard skeleton of Ottoman power continued to be military. Relying upon the hardy peasants of Anatolia for their armies, the Ottoman sultans developed far stronger, more cohesive forces than any ever employed by their Seljuk predecessors. Unwilling as yet to challenge the still-fearsome Mameluke sultanate beyond Asia Minor in Syria, the Ottomans employed these forces against the declining power of the Byzantine Empire in the West.

That empire, though once again ruled by Greeks, had never really recovered from the blow of the fourth Crusade—its rule over the Balkan peoples was now only nominal. The Ottoman Sultan Mohammed II took advantage of this weakness by helping such Balkan peoples as the Bulgars to resist Byzantine authority. In this way he kept his enemies busy supressing rebellions while at the same time cutting them off from Balkan resources and reinforcements. Then, judging the time ripe, in the year 1453 Mohammed II won his title, the Conqueror. He mounted a mighty assault against the city of Byzantium itself, and to the astonishment and horror of all Christendom it fell. This was the final downfall of the Byzantine Empire, Christianity's ancient bulwark in the East. After nearly a thousand years of assault Islam had finally breached the mighty rampart on the Bosphorus—and now all of Europe lay open to Moslem invasion through the undefended Balkans. It was this dreadful fact which sobered European rejoicing over the victory in Spain.

A few decades after the Ottoman capture of Byzantium (which the conquerors rebuilt as the city of Istanbul) the economic base of Mameluke power in Syria, already badly damaged by Tamerlane's invasion in 1400, was dealt another and this time mortal blow. For in May 1498 a daring Portuguese sea captain named Vasco da Gama sailed his caravel all the way around the tip of southern Africa into the Indian Ocean and then on to India itself. Loading his vessel with precious silks and spices, da Gama returned by the same route to Lisbon. There his cargo showed a handsome profit for the Portuguese monarch who had financed the voyage, Prince Henry the Navigator. Western Europe had at last discovered the sea route by which it could trade directly with the Orient, bypassing Near Eastern middlemen. This meant eventual ruin for the merchants of Syria and Egypt—and a subsequent decline in taxable wealth for the Mameluke sultans.

Of course the Mamelukes attempted to fight off the Portuguese threat—but in vain. Their fleets were mainly composed of thin-skinned, oar-propelled galleys meant to do battle on the relatively smooth waters of the Mediterranean and Red seas. They proved to be no match for the large, stoutly built sailing ships of Portuguese admirals used to navigating the gale-blown North Atlantic. Within a remarkably short time Portuguese vessels dominated the Indian Ocean and penetrated the Persian Gulf and the Rea Sea with impunity. Later the Dutch, and later still the English, were to follow the Portuguese to the southern shores of Asia and seize for themselves the rich commerce of the Orient.

The Ottoman Empire

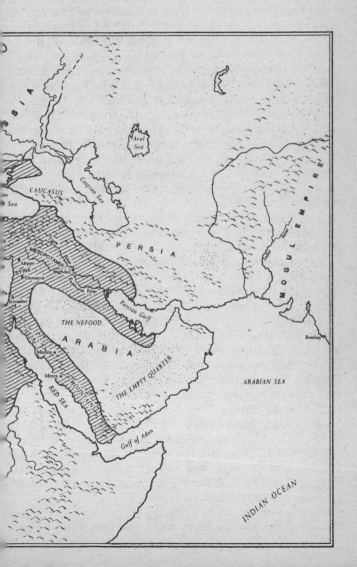

This European eruption into the Indian Ocean occurred at the same time that Spanish ships were cautiously exploring the islands and coasts of new trans-
atlantic lands they mistakenly believed to be the out-
lying provinces of Cathay. Indeed, the Genoese pirate
Cristoforo Colombo had received his commission to lead
the first of these voyages of discovery from Ferdinand
and Isabella on that very field of Santa Fe where the
Catholic Monarchs were still celebrating the fall of
Granada. All of which meant in the long run that European commerce and civilization were about to expand
far beyond that Mediterranean-centered region which
for thousands of years had been its focus. The days
were fast approaching when the Islamic nations bor-
dering the Mediterranean were to decline into economic stagnation.

But those days were not just yet. For nearly two
centuries after the voyages of da Gama and Colombo
the Mediterranean world retained something of its old
importance and vigor. In Islam that vigor inspired the
Ottoman Turks to new conquests. Mohammed II had
captured Byzantium and spread influence deep into the
Balkans; his grandson, Selim I (known as the Stern
and Inflexible), turned Ottoman power to the east and
south. In 1514 he invaded Persia, inflicting a crushing
defeat on the Shia Shah Ismail of that land and adding
Upper Mesopotamia and Kurdistan to the Ottoman
Empire. Then he marched against the Mamelukes, who
had unwisely allied themselves with Shah Ismail. In
1516 Selim's armies advanced into Syria where, at the
great battle of Marj Dabiq, north of Aleppo, they utterly
crushed the Mameluke forces. A few months later, in
January of 1517, Selim followed up this victory by advancing into Egypt, where he captured the city of Cairo.
Tuman Bey, the last Mameluke sultan, was beheaded
by Selim's executioner.

Selim's successor, Sulaiman I (called by his subjects
the Lawgiver and by Europeans the Magnificent) saw

that the key to further conquest along the shores of the Mediterranean was maritime. He accordingly developed a mighty navy, the most powerful ever to sail those waters. With this fleet he was able to bring under Ottoman rule the entire North African shore including the port cities of Tunis, Tripoli, Algiers, and Oran. These territories were eventually to be organized into the *ojaks* (regencies) of Algeria, Tunisia, and Libya with roughly the same borders they have today. Ottoman Turkish governors were appointed who ruled primarily through already established local dynasties and administrations. Only the distant Atlantic kingdom of Morocco maintained its independence from Ottoman rule—but at the price of closing itself off entirely, like ancient Japan, from the outside world.

The introduction of a new, dynamic power into the disintegrated Moslem world of North Africa had an unlooked-for result across the Strait of Gibraltar. There for many years the Spanish monarchy had busied itself with the "purification" of its domains, which meant the massacre, expulsion, and forced conversion of those hundreds of thousands of Jews and Moslems left behind in the ruins of al-Andalus. Catholic Spain was simply continuing the Reconquista—now through the dreadful engines of the Holy Inquisition. For a while Moslems and Jews who professed conversion to Catholicism were spared; but with the rise of the Ottoman threat in North Africa even the converts were expelled. Many took refuge in Ottoman lands, bringing with them valuable skills, crafts, and scientific knowledge. Indeed, when one of his advisors commented on the statesmanship of Ferdinand, Sulaiman the Magnificent replied, "What! Call ye this Ferdinand wise who depopulates his own domains to enrich mine?"

Sulaiman's fleets continued to be the scourge of the Mediterranean during his lifetime. But in 1571 Don Juan of Austria (half brother of Spain's King Philip II)

gathered together the navies of Spain, Venice, and
Genoa and at the great battle of Lepanto sank more
than three hundred of the fearsome Ottoman war galleys. A short time before that disaster the Ottomans
had captured the island of Cyprus. When news of the
defeat at Lepanto was brought to the sultan in Istanbul, he merely commented, "When the Venetians sank
my fleet they only singed my beard. It will grow again.
But when I captured Cyprus I cut off one of their arms."
But the sultan was a little too optimistic. It was true
that the Ottomans rebuilt their navy, but after Lepanto
it was never again to be a controlling force in the Mediterranean. In the Black Sea, however, Turkish naval
power remained supreme—and through it the Ottomans were able to capture much of the Russian Crimean coast.

At its greatest extent the Ottoman Empire stretched
from India to Morocco, from the Sudan far into the
Balkans. For the successors of Sulaiman slowly pushed
northward until they had brought all of Greece and
present-day Bulgaria, Romania, Hungary, and most of
Yugoslavia under their sway. Twice the Ottoman armies even hammered on the gates of Vienna, but they
were finally thrown back by the Polish King John So-
bieski in 1683. This penetration into the European
heartland marked the utmost advance of the Ottoman
tide, which thereafter slowly receded.

The fact that all of the earlier Arab Empire was now
ruled by Turks leads us to a vexing problem of definition. In these pages we are recounting the history of
the Arab world—but who are Arabs? During the first
centuries following the death of the Prophet that question was easily answered: they were people in or from
Arabia. Yet, as we have seen, the original Arab conquerors soon merged with their subject peoples until
they were all but indistinguishable from Persians,
Egyptians, Syrians, or North Africans. True, the nomadic desert tribesmen of central Arabia, remaining
beyond the control of Fatimids, Abbasids, Seljuks, or

Ottomans, retained their "pure" identity. But the
wastelands of Arabia hardly constitute what anyone
would define as the Arab world. Nor is that world coex-
tensive with the religion of Islam; for that huge domain
of faith includes hundreds of millions of Indians, East
Indians, Chinese, Central Asiatics, and black Africans
whom no one would call Arabic. So for our purposes we
shall define the Arab world as that area in which the
Arabic language (or some modified version of it) is still
spoken and where the people—be they Syrian, Egyptian, Iraqi, North African, or other—still consider
themselves the children of Arabic culture.

This definition is of some importance here, precisely
because the Ottoman Turks were not, and never considered themselves to be, part of the Arab world. True,
some of the Ottoman sultans could speak more than a
smattering of Arabic, but many of them spoke better
French and English. True, they were devout Moslems,
but the sultans also considered themselves the "pro-
tectors" of millions of Christian subjects. The truth was
that the Ottoman Empire was a cosmopolitan regime
whose rulers looked upon *all* its peoples—Bulgars,
Egyptians, Greeks, Syrians, Romanians, Persians,
Slavs, Tunisians, Lebanese, Jews, and Arabs—as *subject* nations to be governed from, and for the benefit of,
the Turkish homeland in Asia Minor. To Arabs, as to
Europeans, the Ottoman Turks were, essentially, foreign masters.

To be sure, certain special restrictions were carried
over from those long-gone days of purely Arab ascendancy in Islam: Christians and Jews had to pay a special
poll tax, they were not allowed to ride horses and were
forbidden to bear arms, and the Ottoman civil service
was closed to them. But in practice these distinctions
between Arab and non-Arab Ottoman subjects were of
little import. As time passed, taxes of all kinds grew
heavier and heavier for everybody, so that the special
poll tax became a relatively insignificant burden. Although Christians and Jews might not work their way

up through the ranks of government, many found
places of distinction as advisors at the top. And the
prohibition against bearing arms was, under the Ottomans, a blessing.

A new Ottoman Turk ruling class of governors and
administrators was imposed on the Arab provinces of
the Empire as well as upon the Christian; but unlike
the Mamelukes these officials did not generally settle
down in a subject province and adopt it as their homeland. The Sublime Porte (as the Ottoman capital at
Istanbul was called, after the great gate of the royal
palace) made it a policy to frequently shift its officials
from post to post; when they retired, they usually returned to Turkey (as Asia Minor came to be known).
So there was for a very long time no question of any
attempted "Turkification" of the Arab world. Turkish
was the language of government, but Arabic remained
the language of knowledge and the basic vernacular
of Syrians, Egyptians, North Africans, and all the other
settled peoples of Western Islam. And as time passed,
a very large share of local political power passed into
the hands of local, provincial ruling classes. Aside from
taxes the burden of Turkish rule was for centuries more
psychological than practical.

Yet modern Arabs almost universally regard their
four centuries of subjection to the Ottoman Turks as
a dark and shameful period in their history. This is
due primarily to their vivid sense of past greatness. As
the American historian W. C. Smith has observed, "The
Arab sense of bygone splendor is superb. One cannot
begin to understand the modern Arab if one lacks a
perspective feeling for this. In the gulf between him
and, for instance, the modern American, a matter of
prime significance has been precisely the deep differ-
ence between a society with a memory of past greatness, and one with a sense of present greatness." To
which one may add that the Arab view of the Ottoman
Turks depended also upon the valor and efficiency with
which these foreign rulers defended Islam against the

resurgent tide of Christendom; it was only in the latter days of the Ottoman Empire, when those defenses crumbled, that real hostility between Arabs and Turks emerged.

But even before the Christian invasions of Islam during the nineteenth century the decay of Ottoman rule was far progressed. There were various reasons for this. First of all there was degeneration at the top— the abilities of the ruling sultans declined steadily from the great days of Selim and Sulaiman the Magnificent. This was in large part due to the way the succession to the throne was arranged. During the early days of the Empire it was customary for Ottoman sultans to make their sons provincial governors, so that when one of these ascended to the sultanate he had already a great deal of administrative experience. But the sultans, with several wives and many concubines, always had a surplus of sons, and these would often fight for possession of the throne. Sultan Mohammed II, the Conqueror, solved this problem by issuing a decree that required his successor to slaughter all his brothers when he became sultan. Thus when Mohammed III reached the throne in 1595, he celebrated his elevation by murdering all nineteen of his brothers. Afterward a different system was adopted—all heirs or potential heirs to the throne were raised in semi-isolation, in special pavilions within the royal palace. The result was that when one of them became sultan, he lacked any experience of government.

Another and even stranger reason for Ottoman decay was the system whereby the sultan maintained his armies. Originally, Ottoman forces had been composed of free-born Turks and other Moslems. But as the Empire expanded and Turkish warriors settled down to enjoy the fruits of their conquests, a new source of recruits was found through slavery. Now the teachings of Islam frowned upon slavery as a detestable institution, but they recognized its existence. Moslems were not to enslave other Moslems nor even their infidel (non-Moslem) subjects. Only those infidels who actively fought against Islam and were subsequently captured in battle were subject to enslavement. Ottoman sultans, urgently in need of soldiers to defend and garrison their vast domains (and, as the commerce of the Near East declined, increasingly unable to pay mercenaries), broke this traditional law. They took to enslaving the children of their Christian subjects—Bulgars, Albanians, Greeks, Serbs, Slavs, and Armenians. These children became the absolute property of the sultan himself. The more promising among them were educated in special palace schools to be government administrators or servants in the royal household. The rest were enlisted into the Ottoman standing infantry, the famous corps of Janissaries (from the Turkish *yeni-cheris* or new troops). This of course ensured the outrage and undying hatred of the sultan's Christian subjects, while generating deep resentment among the Moslems upon whom the Janissaries were garrisoned. Worst of all, since the Janissaries were loyal to and dependent upon the sultan alone and not his government, they became a kind of dangerous armed guard enforcing the ruler's personal incompetence.

But of course the main reason for the decline of Ottoman power was simply the fact that it existed principally in the Near East and North Africa—regions that, as we have seen, were rapidly becoming economic backwaters. And this general decline was occurring just at the time when Western Europe, energized by the expansion of world trade through the Age of Discovery, was beginning to evolve toward industrialization.

Historians have argued endlessly as to why Islam did not develop those capitalist and industrial institutions which became the basis of European power. It has been suggested that there is something inherently antitechnological in Moslem doctrine or antiprogressive in the Arab character. But, as we have shown, there was certainly never anything antiscientific or anti-intellectual in Islamic culture. One need not seek the seeds of the Arab world's decay in such problematic theories; one has only to look upon the ruins and deserts of the Near East and North Africa created by ages of warfare and barbarian invasions to comprehend that the basic resources for industrialization required by eighteenth- and nineteenth-century technology were lacking.

And as Ottoman administration and economic power degenerated, so too did local law and order, public finance, roads, waterways, postal services, harbors, irrigation systems, public health, and finally even the bedrock of agriculture upon which Moslem society rested. This steady, general decay of a once mighty culture was deeply humiliating to Arab scholars and intellectuals. It led them to seek perhaps too much consolation and guidance in the study of past glories, and to develop a defensively touchy contempt for the new technology wielded like a weapon by Christendom. The world of Islam turned inward, away from an impoverished present, and so stagnated into helplessness before a threatening future.

The first signal of the decline of Ottoman military power came, as we have seen, before the gates of Vienna in 1683. During the next century the sultans were defeated three times by the emerging European power of Imperial Russia. In 1774 they were forced to grant political independence to their Tartar subjects and hand over their Crimean territories to the Russian Empress Catherine the Great. As an added humiliation the Sublime Porte was required to recognize Russia's right to "protect" Greek and Russian Orthodox Christians within the Ottoman Empire.

Another early example of how the nations of the Arab world were declining into mere pawns in the game of European power politics occurred when in 1798 the young French general Napoleon Bonaparte descended on Egypt with a powerful army. He easily routed the Egyptian Janissaries, but his purpose was

The Sick Man of Europe

not to make war on the Ottomans; it was to strike a blow against the French Republic's arch-foe, England, by cutting the Red Sea route to Britain's commercial empire in India. Yet, as he later confessed to a friend, Napoleon had more than that in mind. "I saw myself founding a new religion," he said, "marching into Asia, riding on an elephant, a turban on my head and in my hand a new Koran that I would have composed to suit my needs." Indeed, in pursuit of such fantasies the conqueror had brought with him scores of botanists, astronomers, archaeologists, and cartographers. Their great work, the *Description d'Egypte*, aroused world interest in that ancient land. Napoleon even planned to cut a canal at the isthmus of Suez to ensure "the free and exclusive possession of the Red Sea for the French Republic." All these dreams vanished when British Admiral Lord Horatio Nelson arrived with a battle fleet and chased the French away.

In the meantime the outraged sultan at Istanbul had dispatched a formidable army (composed mainly of Albanian troops) to Egypt to restore his authority there against the French, the British, and all other interlopers. It arrived in 1799. Among its officers was a young man of outstanding ability named Mohammed Ali. He soon sized up the situation in Cairo; the French and British between them had destroyed the power of the local Ottoman authorities (which in any event had been hateful to the Egyptians), and there thus existed an opportunity. Mohammed Ali boldly seized his chance and took control of the local government. By 1805 the Ottoman sultan had no choice but to recognize him as khedive (viceroy) of Egypt.

With the energy of genius, Mohammed Ali began to transform his newly won domain. He started new irrigation projects to harness the Nile River, invited European experts to teach the new technology in Egyptian schools, started (with Western help and advice) a small manufacturing industry, and built a powerful new army. In 1811 at the sultan's orders he used this army to quell a rebellion among the Wahhabi tribes of Arabia; in 1820 he marched south to conquer much of the Sudan; in 1827, again at the sultan's invitation, Mohammed Ali's forces attempted to put down an uprising in Greece. But here they were defeated by English and Russian intervention; the Greeks won their independence from the Ottoman Empire in 1832. Shortly thereafter Mohammed Ali seized control of Syria and made his own son, Ibrahim Pasha, governor there. The sultan, cowering in Istanbul, was forced to ask the hated Russians for help in stemming Mohammed Ali's ambitions.

This, however, thoroughly alarmed Great Britain. All during the nineteenth century England's rival on India's northwest frontier was Russia. It was basic English policy to prevent Russian expansion south, either in central Asia or in the Near East (where such expansion would threaten the route to India). British politicians had gradually come to realize that their cheapest defense against Russian penetration of the Near East was a strong Ottoman bulwark. Now that bulwark was threatened with disintegration through the ambitions of Mohammed Ali—and it was the Russians who were hastening to help the sultan! English Foreign Minister Lord Palmerston hastily called a conference of leading European powers to avert "chaos" in the Near East. Through threats and diplomacy, by 1841 he had persuaded Austria, Russia, and Prussia to join England in the Treaty of London, which declared the "Egyptian Question" to have been solved. The solution was to force Mohammed Ali to give up Syria to the sultan, retire to Egypt, and accept a limit of 18,000 men to his army (which had numbered 150,000). On the other hand he was permitted to retain the title viceroy of Egypt and to found a dynasty that was to last until 1952.

What this entire episode dramatically confirmed was that European military power, founded upon industrialization, could now easily intervene anywhere in the

Arab world. Only the jealousies and conflicting ambitions of the European nations kept them from seizing parts of that world at will. Indeed, only by playing one Christian power off against another was the Ottoman Empire now able to survive at all.

And as Islam's frontiers in the Near East were breached, so too was its remaining power in the West swept aside. There, since the days of the Catholic Monarchs, Spain and Portugal had carried their war against the Moslems to the North African coast. At various times they seized such port cities as Tangiers, Algiers, Tunis, and Tripoli; but by the seventeenth century, with the help of the Ottomans, local forces had recaptured these places. The answer of North African Arabs to Spanish and Portuguese raids was to wage a prolonged war against the shipping of any and all Christian nations in the Mediterranean. This seagoing guerrilla warfare soon degenerated into outright piracy and became the mainstay of the economics of the Barbery (Berber) Coast states. Divided by the Ottomans into three regencies, Algeria, Tunisia, and Tripoli were essentially maritime city states. Their pirates were the scourge of the Mediterranean, and into their slave pens thousands of unfortunate Christian seamen and passengers were dragged yearly to await ransom or sale. It would be well to remember, however, that in those days North African Moslems who fell into Christian hands were also sold into slavery through the great markets of Pisa or Genoa.

In Tunis in 1705 a Turkish general of the Janissary corps named Hussein Bey seized local power. Although he vaguely acknowledged Ottoman authority, he established his own dynasty, which lasted until 1957. At about the same time a similar dynasty was founded in Tripoli by Ahmad Caramanli. But in Algeria, the strongest of the Barbary states, events took a different turn. After a series of ever feebler Ottoman governors (most of whom were assassinated), the Algerians established a republic, with a president called the dey who was appointed for life. The deys had to cope with wild tribes in the interior, with Ottoman Janissary garrisons, and also with the corporation of pirates whose sea plundering provided most of the national income. It is small wonder then that of the twenty-eight deys who ruled until the mid-nineteenth century no less than fourteen were murdered.

The Christian powers dealt with the pirate nations of North Africa in a variety of ways. Some arranged treaties whereby in return for the payment of yearly tribute their ships and citizens would be immune to molestation. Others waged an endless and ineffective battle against the pirates. The truth was that the entire North African coast was the lair of lawlessness and beyond the control of anyone, even of its native rulers. Treaties and agreements between these and the Christian nations were constantly being violated and breaking down.

It was to protect the ships and citizens of the newly founded American republic from the Moslem pirates of the Mediterranean that, at the beginning of the nineteenth century, the United States organized its first national navy. American squadrons of sailing vessels waged an off-and-on war against Algeria, Tunis, and Tripoli for several years—sinking pirate ships when encountered, blockading and bombarding their home ports when possible. At one point during the war against Tripoli (1801-1805) a company of United States Marines led by one William Eaton marched on Tripoli from the Libyan desert, attempting to foment a revolution against the ruling viceroy, Yusuf Caramanli. It was during his march "to the shores of Tripoli" that General Eaton solemnly informed a group of Bedouin sheikhs that God had provided a separate heaven for Americans—but they would be permitted to visit the Moslem paradise in small groups if they wished. The sheikhs were vastly amused by this but doubted that Eaton would be permitted into paradise unless he became a devout Moslem. Eaton's adventure failed in the end; but the new American frigates were so effective against the pirates that by 1815 American shipping was safe throughout the Mediterranean. The following year, having triumphantly concluded her prolonged wars against Napoleonic France, England dispatched a powerful battle fleet to North Africa under the command of Admiral Lord Exmouth. That fleet leisurely bombarded the pirate ports into ruins—and North African piracy thereafter ended.

Meanwhile the French had built up a very profitable trade with North Africa based on a French trading post at Bône in Algeria. But the French were not always prompt in their commercial payments. In 1830 Husein, the dey of Algiers, called in the French consul to discuss with him a much-delayed payment owed by French merchants to two Algerian Jewish wheat dealers. The dey informed the consul that unless that debt was paid immediately, he would not permit the French to continue trading from Bône. According to witnesses the consul replied with words "of a very gross and irritating nature." The dey grew angry and struck the French consul lightly two or three times with a feathery fly whisk he was holding.

This outrageous, towering, apocalyptic insult to the honor of France was answered by immediate invasion. Hundreds of French transports debarked thousands of soldiers who promptly set about the conquest of the entire nation. They did not blush to distribute leaflets to the Algerians that read: "We French, your friends... are going to drive out your tyrants, the Turks, who persecute you, who steal your goods, and never cease menacing your lives.... Follow our advice; it is good advice and can only make you happy."

It soon became apparent that the French intended not merely to make Algerians happy but also to conquer the entire nation permanently, transform its Arab and Berber population into a species of Moslem Frenchmen, and settle many thousands of French citizens upon the land. Later there would even be an attempt

to make Algeria a *département* of metropolitan France.
The French meant to wipe out not only Moslem armies
and rebels, but also Moslem culture.

The "insolent" dey was quickly deposed and his
forces destroyed; but the peasantry of Algeria and the
Berber tribes of the inland provinces rallied to wage
a guerrilla war against France that lasted fifteen years.
Under the command of the notorious General Begeaud
the French "pacified" Algeria with the utmost ferocity.
As the general remarked, "It may be that I shall be
called a barbarian, but ... I consider myself as above
the reproaches of the press." By 1880 Algeria could be
declared safe for European tourists.

With Algeria subdued, French interest turned to
neighboring Tunisia. There in 1860 the local ruler,
Mohammed Bey, had granted a European-style constitution (*destur* in Arabic) to his subjects and instituted many progressive reforms. But all of this was cut
short when on the pretext of punishing some border
bandits the French took over Tunisia in 1879. There
was almost no fighting, and the bey was permitted to
continue as a figurehead for the French administrators
who subsequently governed the country.

Meanwhile at the other end of the Mediterranean
French civilian engineers, under the leadership of Ferdinand de Lesseps and with the agreement and cooperation of Said Pasha, one of Mohammed Ali's sons (to
whom they paid a small fortune for the privilege), were
directing the labor of thousands of Egyptians in the
cutting of the Suez Canal. The work had started in
1859 and was still in progress when Said Pasha died
in 1863. His successor, Ismail Pasha, continued to cooperate with the French until, amid splendid ceremonies, the canal was opened in 1869. It had cost some
thirty thousand Egyptian lives to build; nonetheless
Ismail's government agreed to pay a large sum to the
French company that had overseen construction, and
furthermore to grant the company full rights to run
the canal for ninety-nine years.

Britain, whose imperialist politicians were trying to seize all of East Africa, from Capetown to the Sudan, could not of course regard French control of this new and much shorter route to India with equanimity. But if war with France was to be avoided, England needed a solid pretext for intervening in Egypt. That pretext was provided by the Khedive Ismail's extravagance, which plunged the country into financial ruin. At first in cooperation with the French, later alone, British "advisors" took over much of the administration of public finance in Egypt. This in turn provoked a nationwide rebellion led by an Egyptian Army officer, one Colonel Arabi, under the slogan "Egypt for the Egyptians!" In 1882 a British fleet bombarded Alexandria, and soon thereafter a British expeditionary force landed. Led by General Sir Garnet Wolseley, the English troops utterly routed Arabi's forces at the battle of Tel-el-Kebir and occupied the entire country. Tewfik, the son of Ismail, was confirmed as khedive, but he was no more than a puppet; the government of Egypt was entirely controlled by the English. As for the Suez Canal, that problem was solved by British Prime Minister Benjamin Disraeli, who with the help of the banking firm of Lord Rothschild simply bought out most of the French shareholders in the canal company and presented the waterway to Queen Victoria as a birthday present.

And when in 1898 the tribesmen of the Sudan, following the fanatically religious leadership of a military chieftain who claimed to be the Mahdi (Messiah), threw out their Egyptian masters, a British force under the command of Lord Herbert Kitchener steamed up the Nile and, at the battle of Omdurman, destroyed the Sudanese rebels. Thereafter the Sudan too became a British protectorate.

In 1904 England and France, fearing the rising tide of imperial German militarism and the worldwide, if dimwitted, ambitions of the German Emperor Wilhelm II, came to an informal "arrangement" known as the

Entente Cordiale (Friendly Understanding). Among other matters the Entente put an end to Anglo-French rivalry in Africa by recognizing British control of Egypt in return for projected French control of Morocco. That same year French diplomats concluded a similar deal with Italy; France would grant the Italians a "free hand" in Libya (to which thousands of Italians had already emigrated) in exchange for Italy's noninterference in Morocco. An agreement with Spain, dividing Morocco into a small Spanish "sphere of influence" in the north and a much larger French sphere in the south, completed the diplomatic groundwork. A suitable pretext (restoring law and order) having been found, French forces under the leadership of Marshal Lyautey began occupying various strategic points in Morocco. By 1912 the Moroccan sultan was forced to sign the treaty of Fez, which transformed his ancient kingdom into a French protectorate.

But the French occupation of Morocco was to be different from their conquest of Algeria and Tunis. Morocco had never been part of the Ottoman Empire; at the price of sealing itself off from the world, it had retained independence since the time of the Spanish Reconquista. Its medieval society, unable to offer any resistance to French forces, was also far too "foreign" to be absorbed into French culture. Furthermore, Marshall Lyautey was a colonial statesman of genius who genuinely loved and understood the society over which he presided as France's first resident general. So French occupation rested lightly on Morocco; its sultan was permitted to rule as a figurehead, and its ancient culture was respected.

Now except for Morocco all the European-conquered provinces of North Africa—Algeria, Tunisia, Egypt, and the Sudan—were nominally part of the Ottoman Empire; yet, as we have seen, the Sublime Porte never attempted any effective defense of these regions. This was simply due to the fact that Ottoman power had so decayed as to be all but nonexistent. The Empire was now derisively known throughout Christendom as "the sick man of Europe." Which was also a remarkably apt description of its ruling sultan, Abdul Hamid II ("Abdul the Damned" to his long-suffering subjects), who maintained his power through overflowing prisons, bloody executions, and a corps of thirty thousand spies. After the Zionist leader Theodore Herzl met Abdul Hamid in 1902 (while unsuccessfully trying to buy land in Palestine for Jewish settlement), he confided the following description to his diary: "I can see him before me now, the Sultan of this declining robber empire. Small, shabby, with his badly dyed beard touched up apparently once a week...the feeble hands in their over-sized gloves...the bleating voice, restraint in every word and fear in every glance. And *this* rules!"

As for the Arab world, the dismemberment of the Ottoman Empire meant only an exchange of one set of foreign masters for another. True, Ottoman rule was usually easier than European precisely because of the Empire's decay and inefficiency and because the Turks were, after all, Moslems. But by the beginning of the twentieth century Arab freedom was restricted to the impenetrable deserts of central Arabia. Elsewhere the Arab world was entirely subject to Ottoman misrule or European imperialism. But the seeds of a great Arab awakening had long since been planted; and during the next half-century they would slowly grow once again into Arab independence.

CHAPTER SEVEN

The Dream and the Betrayal

In the Name of God, the Compassionate, the Merciful
By the snorting Chargers!
And those that dash off sparks of fire!
And those that scour to the attack at morn!
...that which is in men's breasts
shall be brought forth...

KORAN, C

Denis de Rivoyre, a Frenchman who traveled extensively throughout the Arab world in 1884, reported: "Everywhere I came upon the same abiding and universal sentiment: hatred of the Turks....An Arab movement, newly risen, is looming in the distance...." M. de Rivoyre's hosts were perhaps too polite to inform him of Arab hatred of those European powers, including France, which had carved their world into colonies. Nor did the French traveler understand that deep as Arab resentment against the Turks might be, so long as Turkish rule remained inefficient and so long as the Sublime Porte was defending Islam, however ineffectively, against Christendom, the subject Arab peoples would hesitate to revolt.

Sultan Abdul Hamid II made what use he could of this ancient pan-Islamic feeling. His predecessors had resurrected the title of caliph, and Abdul tried hard to identify himself as defender of the faithful. From 1901 to 1908 his government constructed a railway from Damascus to Medina—supposedly to facilitate the journey of Moslem pilgrims on their way to Mecca, actually to provide means for Ottoman troops to penetrate the central Arabian deserts and strengthen the sultan's hold on the Bedouin tribes.

Another element of the desperate juggling act whereby Abdul the Damned maintained his power and independence was the modernization of his armies with the help of a German military mission in Istanbul. The threat of German penetration also provided Abdul with a counterweight against British and Russian pressures. The Germans, anxious then as always to promote their everlasting *Drang nach Osten* (drive to the East), happily poured money and experts into the Ottoman domains. "Berlin to Baghdad" became the slogan of German railroad companies eager to open new sources of trade. Kaiser Wilhelm II himself made a visit to Istanbul, Damascus, and Jerusalem (where the Jaffa Gate was enlarged so he could ride through on a white horse). All of which made the British very nervous and spurred them into their Entente Cordiale with France.

But if the Moslem masses remained grumblingly loyal to the sultan, there now arose a reform movement within the Turkish ruling class itself. Originally formed by exiled intellectuals in Paris and Cairo, the Young Turk movement developed strong links with an antisultanate underground in the homeland. By 1906 this underground organization was being joined by Turkish army officers—including a young captain Mustafa Kemal, of whom we will hear much more. In 1908 matters came to a head when the Committee of Union and Progress (CUP), the name chosen by the organized underground, came out into the open and demanded a constitution. Abdul Hamid hesitated, found that his army had mutinied, and hastily caved in. Elections were immediately organized; and on December 17, 1908, a parliament met in Istanbul. When, in April 1909, Abdul the Damned attempted a counterrevolution, he was hanged from a high minaret of his palace.

The Arab subjects of the sultan, who took no part in the so-called Young Turk uprising, nonetheless greeted its triumph enthusiastically. Like the Turkish rebels, they hoped now for a stronger defense against European imperialism; they hoped also for greater local autonomy and equality within the Empire. But these hopes did not quite coincide with Young Turk aims. True, the rebels intended a general liberalization of the old sultanate's tyranny; but they were also fervent Turkish nationalists who intended to maintain the supremacy of the Turkish nation, language, and culture within their domains. One of the Young Turk leaders, Talaat Bey, speaking in 1910, described the constitutional equality of Turkish and non-Turkish peoples as an "unrecognizable ideal."

During the first four years of Young Turk power (1908–1912) all the remaining Ottoman provinces in Europe were lost, except for a small area around Istanbul. Bulgaria declared her independence and the Austro-Hungarian Empire seized Bosnia and Herzegovina. The Italians invaded Libya, which they conquered up to the Egyptian border, and seized the Dodecanese Islands. Greece took the same opportunity to acquire the island of Crete. These disasters only reinforced Turkish nationalism—which now had no one to exert itself upon except the Arab peoples of Syria, Iraq, Palestine, and Arabia itself. And as the Young Turks introduced greater efficiency into the Ottoman government, this concentration of imperial rule over their Arab subjects became ever sterner. The Turkish writer Ziya Gökalp correctly declared: "One can rightly say that the seeds of the Arab separatist movement began to sprout from the soil of Turkish nationalism from 1909 onwards."

It was during these years just before the First World

War that several Arab secret societies were formed in Paris. Of these the most important was al-Fatat (Young Arab), organized in 1911. Its avowed aims were complete independence for the Arab provinces of the Ottoman Empire. Its unavowed aims included independence for Arabs suffering under French, British, and Italian imperialism as well. Al-Fatat moved its headquarters from Paris to Beirut and then to Damascus in 1912. Its underground membership rapidly increased, and on al-Fatat initiative an Arab National Congress was held in Paris in 1913. Although the great majority of delegates came only from Syria, the Young Turks were forced to at least recognize this congress as a fair representation of Arab interests. The Young Turk political party, the Committee of Union and Progress (CUP), sent representatives to Paris to negotiate and the Arab leaders won an apparent victory. Henceforth Arabic was to be the official language in Arab provinces; Arabs would no longer be conscripted into the Ottoman army for service beyond their own home lands; five Arab governors-general would be appointed and no less than three Arab ministers would join the central government at Istanbul.

But this Arab victory was only apparent; as soon as the congress disbanded, the Young Turks speedily welched on all their promises. Arab resentment and bitterness reached new heights. By 1914 Arab leaders had abandoned all hope of reaching an understanding with the Turks. Realizing now that only through total independence could they achieve their aims, these leaders entered into secret negotiations with the British in Egypt, hoping to enlist England's support for their cause. But the British response was hesitant, lukewarm at best.

Then in August 1914 the shaky edifice of European peace collapsed into the chaos of World War I. England, France, and Russia plunged into a life-and-death struggle against Imperial Germany and Austria-Hungary. Later Italy, Japan, and in 1917 the United States would join the war against Germany. The situation in the Near East was immediately transformed.

For centuries England had propped up "the sick man of Europe" as a defense against Russian expansion to the south, but English governments had never looked upon that fabulous invalid with anything but contempt. Now, although it was well known that the Germans were pressing the Turks to enter the war on their side, England could not bring herself to plead or bargain for Turkish support. The Royal Navy was supreme in the Mediterranean, and that was all the Turks had to know. They knew it all right—Talaat Bey and his cohort Enver Pasha (respectively prime minister and war minister in the new government) had no desire to bring themselves under the guns of that fleet if they could possibly avoid it. True, they had signed a secret treaty of alliance with the Germans; but they might worm out of that by claiming that Germany was the aggressor in this war. At the very least they hoped to delay matters until they could see which way the tide of battle would go.

But matters were brought to a head by a strange chain of circumstances. In 1914 there were two German cruisers in the Mediterranean, the *Geoben* and the *Breslau*. Their mission in case of war was to sink French transports carrying reinforcements from Algeria to Europe. They were of course no match for the powerful British squadron in the Mediterranean, and their mission was understood to be somewhat suicidal. Nonetheless, upon receiving news of Germany's declaration of war on France on August 3 they sailed boldly west, trailed by British warships, which could not open fire upon them simply because England's reluctant government did not officially declare war upon Germany until August 5, two days after France. After an ineffective bombardment of the Algerian port o Bône (the German ships never even sighted the Fren convoys), the *Goeben* and the *Breslau* disappeare the night and fog. Later they were again sighted time steaming *east*. The British squadrons, under orders to guard the French convoys and to make certain that the enemy cruisers did not slip past Gibraltar into the Atlantic, did not really press their pursuit. So long as the *Goeben* and the *Breslau* remained in the eastern Mediterranean, there would be plenty of time to track them down and destroy them.

But the Germans had other ideas. The two cruisers made direct for the Dardanelles, where with Turkish permission they were allowed to pass the forts and mine fields and so drop anchor in the Golden Horn at Istanbul. This was of course a clear violation of Turkish neutrality, and the British ambassador in Istanbul objected furiously. But, as Enver Pasha pointed out to him, there was little the Turkish government could now do, for Istanbul lay undefended beneath the cruisers' guns. Within a few days Turkish neutrality was once against secured, by the expedient trick of having the German officers and crews don Turkish uniforms as their ships were inducted into the Turkish navy! Finally, a few weeks later, growing impatient at Turkish procrastination, the German ships sailed into the Black Sea and bombarded Russian Crimean ports. So the Ottoman Empire was carried kicking and screaming into the war on Germany's side. Perhaps not precisely kicking and screaming, for in November 1914 a German victory seemed certain, but nonetheless reluctantly.

It was now clearly in Britain's interest to support a general Arab uprising against the Turks; and the negotiations between British officers in Cairo and Arab emissaries, which had been allowed to lag, were now urgently revived. The Arab negotiators had been sent by Hussein ibn Ali, the Grand Sharif (Protector) of Mecca, thirty-seventh in line of descent from the prophet himself and titular head of the powerful Hashite (Beni Hashim) clan, traditional lords of the hern Arabian deserts. Held in Istanbul for fifteen as an unwilling guest of Abdul Hamid, Hussein

had been returned to Mecca by the Young Turks—
against whom he immediately began to plot. Though
he commanded no military force to speak of, as a revered religious leader of Islam, Hussein could, the British hoped, proclaim an Arab *jihad* or *Holy* War against
the Ottoman power. Hussein's aim, however, was not
simply to gain Arab independence from the Turks but
to make sure that independence could be maintained
against European imperialists as well. Therefore he
hesitated, extracting promises from the British while
assuring the Turks of his undying support, and waiting
to see how the war would go.

But Hussein was not the only power in Arabia. The
south was largely under the control of Abdul Aziz ibn
Saud, leader of the Saudi family and a long-time rebel
against Turkish rule. On December 15, 1914, ibn Saud
signed a treaty with Britain that, though it gave the
English a large measure of control over his foreign
policy, recognized him as independent king of southern
Arabia. But this blow against the Ottomans was more
theoretical than practical; they had rarely exercised
effective rule anywhere in Arabia, and ibn Saud could
make no military contribution to the British war effort.

Between July 1915 and January 1916 there took
place a decisive exchange of letters between Hussein
and Sir Henry McMahon, British High Commissioner
in Egypt, in which the British promised rather vaguely
to create Hashemite kingdoms in Syria and Iraq. No
mention was made of Palestine, but since Palestine had
always been a part of Syria and not a separate Ottoman
province, this omission meant nothing to Hussein. In
any event McMahon, with that splendidly imperial
view natural to Englishmen of his generation, took
none of these promises too seriously. His letters to
Hussein, couched in the language of the *Arabian
Nights,* were an unintentional insult to Arab intelligence. One, for example, began, "To the excellent and
well-born *Sayid,* the descendant of Sharifs, the Crow

of the Proud, Scion of Mohammed's Tree and Branch of the Quraishite trunk, him of the Exalted Presence and of the Lofty Rank...the lodestar of the Faithful and cynosure of all devout Believers...may his Blessing descend upon the people in their multitudes...."

The total cynicism of Britain's negotiations with the Arabs may be judged by the fact that in May 1916 she concluded with France the Sykes-Picot Agreement (named after the two principal negotiators), which secretly divided the whole of Iraq and Syria into British and French spheres of control after victory should be won.

There was now too a new element in Britain's Near Eastern policy, for abundant oil had been discovered in Persia and along the Persian Gulf coast of Arabia. Its importance was well understood even in 1914, for the British Fleet was going over from coal to oil in the years just before the war. An Anglo-Indian force occupied Basra in Iraq in 1914 largely to ensure the safety of oil supplies from the gulf region, and British businessmen were already establishing what was to become the giant Anglo-Persian Oil Consortium. Arabian oil would become increasingly vital, but in those days the paramount British interest remained the security of the Suez lifeline to India.

That lifeline was threatened during 1915 when one of the Young Turk leaders, Jemal Pasha, led an Ottoman army through Syria and toward the gates of Egypt. Jemal Pasha was thrown back from the Suez Canal, but during his campaign he had discovered the vast extent of the anti-Turkish Arab underground in Syria. He immediately instituted an iron-handed military dictatorship in the region, executing scores of Arab leaders, burning villages, and in general earning his title of *al-Jazzar* (the Butcher). These atrocities and, perhaps more importantly, the news that German troops had joined Jemal and planned to march through

Arabia to the conquest of the Yemen prompted Hussein to act. On June 10, 1916, he raised the flag of Arab revolt and called for *jihad* against the Turks. First Mecca, then the Red Sea coast city of Jedda fell to the Arab rebels—but without British arms and advice, that was about the limit of their abilities.

Both the arms and the advice were on their way through a British temporary captain of intelligence named T. E. Lawrence. The illegitimate son of an Anglo-Irish baronet, Lawrence had spent several years before the war traveling extensively throughout the Near East, studying archaeology and Arabic language and history—and, incidentally, spying on the Turks. Sent on a special mission to the Grand Sharif in conquered Jedda in October 1916, Lawrence quickly sized up Hussein and his family. As he declared in his book about the Arab Revolt, *The Seven Pillars of Wisdom*, 'The Sharif of Mecca, we knew to be aged. I found Abdullah the second son too clever. Ali the first son too clean. Zeid the fourth son too cool. Then I rode upcountry to Feisal the third son and found in him the leader with the necessary fire."

With Lawrence's help Feisal soon became the acknowledged leader of the Arab revolt. Lawrence himself, by mastering the techniques of guerrilla warfare, wearing Arab desert dress, and learning to ride camels, soon became a Bedouin warrior. He was well on his way to earning the title bestowed on him by adoring millions in the West: Lawrence of Arabia. But that title rested in part on myth. For Lawrence had no special love for the Arabs. His primary allegiance was to Britain's imperial ambitions in the Near East. While respecting Arab warriors and traditions, Lawrence used his Bedouin comrades principally to further British, not Arab, ends. If he advocated the creation of an Arab kingdom in Syria, this was simply to forestall French imperial ambitions there after the war should end. I' was always understood by him that any new Ara states in that area would come under British "tute-lage."

The Arab revolt, though strategically important to Britain because it immobilized some thirty thousand Turkish troops along the railway from Damascus to Medina and prevented German penetration to the Red Sea coast, was not decisive in the Near East. What was decisive was the Anglo-Australian expeditionary force sent to that region under the command of General Sir Edmund Allenby. This army advanced from Egypt northward into Palestine with Lawrence's Arab tribes-men acting as right-flank guard. By blowing up Turk-ish rail lines and communications and destroying small detachments of Turkish and German troops when they could, the Bedouin warriors—advancing to the charge on camels, like their all-conquering ancestors—made an important contribution to the Allied capture of Je-rusalem on December 9, 1917. So too did two brigades of Palestinian Jewish soldiers who helped hold open the military "gate" in the Turkish lines through which Allenby poured his fifty thousand Australian horsemen in a charge that destroyed the Turko-German army in Syria. Soon afterward Allenby advanced to Damascus; and since an Anglo-Indian army had meanwhile fought its way up the Euphrates and Tigris rivers to the cap-ture of Baghdad, all of Iraq and southern Syria was now firmly in British hands.

It was during the triumphant year of 1917 that Hus-sein was proclaimed King of the Hejaz (that is to say, northern Arabia) by the English and French. That was in January; but in November of that same year, after the Bolshevik revolutionaries had seized power in Rus-sia, they gleefully published the terms of various Allied secret treaties—including the Sykes-Picot Agreement Hussein thus learned of Anglo-French intentions in Syria and Iraq. And, as if this blow was not sufficient, during that same month of November 1917 the British foreign secretary, Lord Arthur James Balfour, pub-lished a letter to the leaders of the worldwide Jewish

Zionist movement in which he declared Britain's support for "the establishment in Palestine of a National Home for the Jewish People." Although the Balfour Declaration (as it came to be known) carefully modified this promise to add that it was "clearly understood that nothing shall be done which may prejudice the civil and religious rights of existing non-Jewish communities in Palestine," it seemed to Arab leaders that Britain intended nothing less than the creation of a Jewish nation. Since there were at that time only some fifty-five thousand Jews and more than seven hundred thousand Arabs in Palestine, this looked like outright robbery. It's not surprising that as the war came to its close in 1918, with the Allies everywhere triumphant (Turkey capitulated on October 30, twelve days earlier than Germany), British diplomats had their hands full trying to explain Britain's intentions in the Near East to the increasingly suspicious Arabs.

But Hussein, Feisal, and other Arab leaders still clung to one hope. The American President Woodrow Wilson had proclaimed the principle of "self-determination" for all nations and peoples everywhere. This policy, which was to be enshrined in the projected League of Nations, was also one of Wilson's famous Fourteen Points for the creation of a just and lasting peace. So when the Paris Peace Conference opened in January 1919, Feisal (with Lawrence as his advisor) attended as spokesman for the Arabs, not without hope.

He might have saved himself the trip. English Prime Minister David Lloyd George and French Premier Georges Clemenceau had already determined that the Arab world of the Near East would be part of the Allied spoils of victory; their respective governments differed only as to how these spoils should be divided. As for President Wilson, his idealism far outran his grasp of political reality—his influence for the Arab cause would be nil. So the three Allied leaders listened, bemused, while Feisal, who spoke only Arabic, addressed them through his interpreter, Colonel Lawrence. They did not realize that, upon the advice of Lawrence, Feisal was simply reciting the Koran while Lawrence recited his own plan for Arab independence under British tutelage in English. It didn't really matter—the charade over, the Conference turned to more urgent matters.

The tortuous diplomatic maneuverings of France and Britain in the Near East need not embroil us here. Real events in that area immediately after the war were as follows:

1. Hussein's kingdom in northern Arabia was soon conquered by the forces of ibn Saud. The old Sharif of Mecca was driven into exile while Saud became king of the new nation of Saudi Arabia, under British tutelage.

2. Hussein was then proclaimed by al-Fatat to be the rightful king of Syria, but he was driven out by a French expeditionary force that seized the country. In some embarrassment the English finally made him King of Iraq.

3. The old Ottoman province of Syria was divided into four new countries: Syria proper, ruled as a mandated territory by the French; Lebanon, an area long dominated by French interests, which became a separate French mandate, its artificial boundaries carefully drawn to include an equal mix of Christians and Moslems; Palestine, a British mandated territory in which the English promised to fulfill the Balfour Declaration; and Trans-Jordan, a semidesert kingdom created for Hussein's second son, Abdullah, which was for all practical purposes a British colony.

"Mandated territories" were supposedly held by the occupying power (France in Syria and Lebanon, England in Palestine and Iraq) on "trust" from the League of Nations, to be administered for the good of the subject people until such time as these should have attained sufficiently high civilization to rule themselves. The entire mandate system was no more than a sop to

Woodrow Wilson's idealism, a shabby disguise for Great Power imperialism. Thus by 1921 the entire Arab world of the Near East was again under foreign domination.

The same fate might have been meted out to Turkey but for the vision and energy of Mustafa Kemal, a Young Turk army captain. During the war this able soldier had inflicted a heavy defeat upon the Allies when they attempted to reach their faltering Russian ally by driving through the Dardanelles. Now, with his country defeated, the Young Turk government fallen, and Greece (an ally of Britain and France during the war) taking advantage of Turkish weakness to invade Greek-settled parts of Asia Minor with the object of "liberating" these areas from Turkish rule, Kemal organized a new army. With it he managed to hold off the Greeks until by the Treaty of Lausanne in 1923 Turkish sovereignty in Asia Minor and around Istanbul was guaranteed. In October of that same year Kemal became first president of the new Turkish Republic. He at once embarked upon a program of modernization that in the course of the next fifty years was to bring Turkey into the modern world. Part of that program was the secularization of Turkey's Islamic society. In 1924 Kemal abolished the title of caliph, and since that time no man has borne it. It was with excellent reason that this great Turk became known as Mustafa Kemal Ataturk (Father of the Turks). His example inspired nationalist and independence movements throughout the Arab world.

European rule of that world in the years following the First World War was in the grand old imperialist tradition. Raw materials such as Saudi Arabian oil, Syrian tobacco, Algerian wheat, Moroccan coffee and hemp were extracted from the subject territories at low prices set in Paris or London. The low prices were maintained by keeping the wages of Arab labor, and hence Arab living standards, as meager as possible. These raw materials were then sold at a handsome profit either directly or as manufactured goods to the rest of the world—including the Arabs, who were forced to pay high prices for all imports. Native Arab manufacturing (except where this was established and controlled by French or English business interests) was discouraged, and all trade and commerce were monopolized by French or English banks. In short, the wealth, labor, and natural resources of the Arab world were thoroughly exploited for the benefit of a handful of French and British financiers, industrialists, and merchants. While the richest Arab merchants and landowners might be "cut in" on some of the profits of the system as very junior partners, the vast Arab masses were kept in the same abysmal poverty they had suffered under the Turks. Resistance to this brutal exploitation was discouraged by French or British armies of occupation and by large police forces—for the support of which the Arabs themselves were heavily taxed.

Nevertheless resistance did take place on an increasing scale in the years between the two World Wars. The Arab world, writhing in the grip of foreign exploitation, was the scene of bloodshed, assassinations, riots, and rebellions which broke out sporadically as local circumstances inflamed the masses.

In Morocco the Bedouin Rif tribesmen of the Atlas Mountains rose against France and Spain under the leadership of a military genius called Abd El Krim. The suppression of this revolt occupied the French and Spanish Foreign Legions for many years—it was finally put down only in 1934. Algeria and Tunisia remained relatively peaceful (though underground independence movements proliferated), but the Italian colony of Libya was wracked by the rebellion of the Sanussis, another of those Moslem puritanical sects, who were suppressed only when the new Italian dictator, Benito Mussolini, introduced his bloodthirsty fascist methods.

In Egypt, long restive under British control, full-scale revolution broke out in 1919. Though this was suppressed by British troops hastily dispatched from England, unrest and rioting continued. Finally in 1922 England declared Egypt independent, but reserved the right to maintain an army there for the protection of the Suez Canal and to intervene politically in Egyptian affairs whenever she wished. This half-baked "independence" did nothing to calm Egyptian nationalists. Riots, assassinations, bombings, and strikes continued, while behind the facade of the Egyptian khedive (a spoiled sixteen-year-old named Farouk who ascended to the throne in 1933) British advisors continued to rule. During these years a new popular nationalist party called the Wafd (delegation) commanded the loyalty of the Egyptian masses—but since it was dominated by rich landowners, it did not seek to replace Farouk, merely to expel the hated British. Some of the Anglo-Egyptian troubles arose from rivalry over control of the Sudan, once ruled by Egypt but now an integral part of the British Empire. Sudanese nationalists feared the Egyptians even more than they detested the British, but they needn't have worried—England was not about to give up her control of this region lying athwart her route to India. Which was also the basic reason she was unprepared to relax her control of Egypt itself.

The British mandate in Iraq, after years of rioting and rebellion, was relinquished in 1930. But Britain by treaty was to train the Iraqi army, maintain air and naval bases on Iraqi soil, and defend Iraq against foreign invasion. This last concession was not for the benefit of the Iraqis but rather for the security of the Iraq Petroleum Company, a consortium of British, American, and French corporations that were now exploiting the nation's oil reserves. Thenceforth Iraq was to be troubled by various army rebellions—directed partly against the Hashemite monarchy founded by Hussein (which, however, survived), partly against British tutelage (which also survived), and partly against the economic imperialism of the petroleum corporations.

Trans-Jordan remained from 1920 to 1939 a kind of nonstate, ruled by King Abdullah and his descendants but entirely dependent on British money, resources, power, and advice for its continued existence. The Jordanian Arab Legion was staffed mostly by English officers and commanded by General Sir John Bagot Glubb, another of those British Arabicists who, under the title Glubb Pasha, continued something of the Lawrence of Arabia tradition.

The French experience in Syria and Lebanon paralleled that of the British in Iraq. Despite France's self-proclaimed "civilizing mission" in the Near East, Syrian and Lebanese nationalists were never reconciled to French rule. Riots, bloody suppressions, and political terrorism marked the years of the French mandate. In 1936 the French signed a treaty with Syrian and Lebanese nationalists that granted independence to both nations (though French military predominance in both regions was to be maintained), but the treaty was never ratified in Paris. With the growing threat of German resurgence under Hitler facing her across the Rhine, France did not feel she could relinquish anything anywhere.

The fate of Palestine during the years between the wars is a matter of such complexity and importance that we will deal with it in a later chapter. Here we will only remark that of all the mandated Arab territories, its history during this time was the bloodiest and most troubled.

So as Europe once again plunged into war in 1939, the Arab world remained everywhere, to greater or lesser degree, in thrall to European imperialism. The high hopes of 1918 had long since been dashed; betrayal was complete. The dream of Arab independence had become a nightmare of imperialist exploitation.

CHAPTER EIGHT

Passage of Fire

In the Name of God, the Compassionate, the Merciful
Fight, therefore, on God's path: lay not burdens
on any but thyself; and stir up the faithful.
The might of the infidels haply will God restrain.

KORAN, LVII

When Americans recall the stirring events of World
War II in the Near East, North Africa, and the Mediterranean, they are likely to remember German General Erwin Rommel, the "Desert Fox," whose dashing
Afrika Korps stormed across the Egyptian deserts to
the very gates of Cairo and Suez; they remember British General Bernard Montgomery's tough "Desert
Rats," who gobbled up entire Italian armies and finally
smashed German ambitions at the great battle of El
Alamein. They think of the tremendous Anglo-American invasion convoys that descended upon Morocco
and Algeria in 1942, of the American defeat at Kas-
serine Pass in Tunisia, and of American redemption
under the flaming will of General George "Blood-and-
Guts" Patton. They remember the decisive British naval victory over the Italian fleet at Taranto, the land-
ings in Sicily, the gallant defense of Malta, the long,
bitter struggle up the spine of Italy, and the fall of

Rome and of Mussolini. Above all they recall that these events were all part of a life-and-death fight between democracy and civilization on the one hand and tyranny, racism, and barbarism on the other. For them the great victory over Nazism and fascism remains the central event of the twentieth century, without which no subsequent world can even be imagined.

The Arab peoples, however, do not recall the Second World War in the same way. For although their homelands were often the scene of mighty battles, the Arabs themselves took but little part in the conflict. To many of them the war conjures memories of imprisonment by British or French or American forces, riots, uprisings, martial law, and humiliation. The war itself must have seemed simply another in that endless series of wars through which the Western powers have determined which of them would impose its imperialistic control over the rest of mankind. In this respect from the Arab viewpoint there seemed little to choose between Allied and Axis powers, for Arabs had suffered conquest and occupation by both. Indeed, many Arabs hoped that a German-Italian victory would liberate them by destroying the might of the French and British empires. Very few Arabs understood the real nature of Nazism or of Hitler's racial policies. They did not foresee that in the event of a Nazi victory their enslavement to Germany would have been a thousand times worse than anything they had suffered at Allied hands. Nor did they comprehend that to Hitler Arabs were Semites just like Jews—and would have endured their own holocaust. This all-but-unbridgeable gap between the past as seen by Arabs and the past as viewed by the West burdens relations between them to this very day.

British policy in the Near East during World War II (to which American policy generally conformed) cannot be understood except in the light of one paramount fact: England deemed control of the Mediterranean and of the Arab world to be vital to her very existence. Indeed, British Prime Minister Winston Churchill declared the defense of that region second in importance only to the defense of the British Isles and, though England still feared a German cross-channel invasion, went so far as to dispatch badly needed supplies and reinforcements to Egypt in the fall of 1940. England would do anything to maintain herself in the Near East, and in this policy she was supported by the United States after 1941. "Anything" included not only the suppression of all Arab rebels but also, when necessary, fighting against her own friends and allies to ensure security in that area.

This tragic complication arose when in June 1940 Hitler's mighty Panzer divisions drove the British into the Channel at Dunkerque and then turned to crush the life out of the French Third Republic. As part of a humiliating armistice forced upon the vanquished the Nazis dictated the establishment of a small French state south of Paris which came to be informally known (from the name of its capital) as "Vichy France." This helpless remnant of France, hardly more than a German puppet state, was ruled by the very old, very authoritarian World War I hero, Marshal Henri Pétain. But many French people refused to accept the German victory as final—and rallied to the "Free French" forces of General Charles de Gaulle in London. Both of these rival French "governments" claimed the allegiance of that vast French overseas empire which remained for the moment beyond Hitler's grasp.

In truth, although supporting the Free French with money and supplies, the English did not much care who controlled France's overseas possessions provided that these did not fall under German authority and that they cooperated with British strategy when required. Regarding German control of Vichy France, however, Britain was exceedingly nervous—she was fighting for her very life; and when, for example, it

The Near East During World War II

appeared that the Vichy French fleet anchored in North African ports might be turned over to the Nazis, the Royal Navy did not hesitate to bombard and sink a French squadron at Mirs El Kebir Bay in Morocco. But Britain was reluctant to directly attack those parts of the French empire under Vichy authority for fear of provoking direct German military intervention. This was especially true of North Africa and the Near East, because any trouble anywhere in the Arab world might just provoke an uprising throughout Islam against Britain as well as France.

In the Near East trouble started when in May 1941 the Vichy government allowed German planes to use Syrian airfields on their way to supply Arab nationalists in Iraq, who were rebelling against British authority. As soon as she had quelled the Iraqi uprising, Britain responded by launching an invasion of Syria and Lebanon with mixed British–Free French forces. Fighting was bitter on the approaches to Damascus and in the city of Beirut; but by July 14, 1941, the local Vichy French authorities surrendered. Syria and Lebanon now passed under the control of de Gaulle's Free French government-in-exile. But Arab nationalists in those lands were not satisfied with this substitution; they demanded full independence. The Free French, like the Vichy French before them, remained unyielding; the usual riots, bombings, "police actions," political terrorism against French rule followed.

De Gaulle's policy in the Near East was to maintain as much control as possible and stall any real decisions until the Free French were strong enough to impose their will independently. But when that day came, after Germany's surrender in Europe in May 1945, the French leader found he had badly misjudged the situation. World opinion would not tolerate the reimposition of French colonial rule. When French troops landed to reinforce their comrades in Syria and Lebanon, Great Britain, with the full support of the

United States and the rest of the newly created United
Nations, ordered their immediate withdrawal. After a
futile bombardment of Damascus the French reluctantly caved in under international pressure and by
July 1945 had handed over local authority to Syrian
and Lebanese nationalists. A year later, during the
summer of 1946, all French and British forces in those
two countries were withdrawn. The mandate was
ended, and two of the most important Arab nations had
at last achieved full independence.

During the war the situation in Iraq, which had
provoked British intervention in Syria and Lebanon in
the first place, was complex and delicate. Iraq, it will
be recalled, had enjoyed nominal independence since
the end of the British mandate in 1930. But it was
allied to Britain by treaty; and its government, led by
Prime Minister Nuri Said, accepted British bases on
its territory and British "tutelage" in its affairs. When
Britain reeled before German might in 1940, a group
of ultranationalist Iraqi army officers thought they saw
an opportunity to rid themselves of the hated British
presence. Led by an aristocrat named Rashid Ali Gai-
lani, they forced the resignation of Nuri Said in March
1940. Then they began cautiously negotiating for German support. This provoked the British to seize Basra
with an Indian force and invade Iraq from Trans-Jordan with Glubb Pasha's Arab Legionnaires during the
spring of 1941. The Iraqi army regime was overthrown,
Rashid Ali sent off to prison, and Nuri Said restored
to power. Thereafter Iraq cooperated with the British
war effort (she declared war on Germany in 1943) and
provided the necessary base from which British forces
(in cooperation with Soviet armies) invaded Iran to
ensure the continued "benevolent" neutrality of that
oil-rich land. So at war's end in 1945 Iraq continued
to remain "independent"—but with British influence
paramount in her affairs. Real independence was to
come some years later.

Egypt was the cornerstone of British control of the Near East, and her cooperation during the war was absolutely essential to the defense of the Suez Canal. Britain did not, however, require the Egyptians to declare war on Germany, because it suited her to maintain Cairo and Alexandria as "neutral" open cities, free from German bombing. But when Italy entered the war on Germany's side in June 1940, matters grew grimmer. The British army easily disposed of the Italians in Libya, and British authorities in Cairo insisted that King Farouk intern Italian nationals in Egypt and dismiss known German sympathizers from his armed forces. This the king was reluctant to do. Many Egyptians were hoping for German victory, not out of any sympathy for Nazism but because it would drive the British from their country. One of these, incidentally, was a young Egyptian army officer, Captain Anwar Sadat, who was caught spying for the Germans and imprisoned by the British.

The Anglo-Egyptian showdown came early in 1942 when Rommel's Afrika Korps drove the British desert army from Libya and western Egypt back upon its last defense line before Cairo. In Rome Mussolini's tailors were designing a new and glorious uniform for the Italian dictator to wear when he entered the Egyptian capital on a white charger; in Cairo itself anti-British mobs roamed the streets chanting "Rommel, Rommel, Rommel." It was even rumored that a suite had been reserved for the victorious German commander at Cairo's famous Shepheard's Hotel. Under these circumstances what would the fat, petulant, dimwitted King Farouk do? The British feared he would seize his opportunity to appoint a pro-German government. Therefore on February 2, 1942, Farouk's palace was surrounded by British tanks. The tall, domineering British ambassador, Sir Miles Lampson, shouldered his way into Farouk's presence and demanded that the king immediately appoint a new, pro-British government— or abdicate. Farouk fluttered, wept, and then did as he

was told. But although this assured total Egyptian sub-
servience to British wishes for the rest of the war (especially after Rommel had been thrown back), the
king's performance utterly destroyed any remaining
Egyptian confidence in the monarchy.

That confidence had in any event long been eroding
through the propaganda of numerous Egyptian underground nationalist organizations. Perhaps the most
powerful of these was the Moslem Brotherhood, founded
in 1920 by a high school teacher as a religious revival
movement. The Brotherhood demanded that Egyptian
society be recognized top to bottom in strict accor-
dance with the precepts of the Koran and ancient Islamic
tradition. The Brotherhood's secret branches proliferated during the years between the wars; and as it came
under increasing attack by the British and their puppet
Egyptian governments, it turned from purely religious
to political activism. The Brotherhood also organized
paramilitary terrorist groups that during the war years
carried out bombings, assassinations, and other anti-
British, anti-Farouk violence.

In the political turmoil and awakening fostered by
Brotherhood activities during the 1930s, Egyptian high
school students played a leading role, especially in
street demonstrations. One of these was a tall, rather
grave teenager named Gamal Abdel Nasser. Nasser's
family had long been *fellaheen* (peasants) working their
tiny farms along the banks of the Nile, but Nasser's
father escaped this grinding poverty when he managed
to secure a job as a postal clerk. Gamal himself was
born at Alexandria in 1918, and by 1935 he was involved in student protest movements and was slightly
wounded by police bullets during the riots of that year.
Those same bullets killed two of his fellow demonstra-
tors. Yet Gamal did not join the Moslem Brotherhood;
for he was already a voracious reader of history and
political biography, and his studies convinced him that
the Brotherhood's aims were outdated: twentieth-
century Egypt could not be rebuilt as an eighth-century

caliphate. In 1937, at the age of nineteen, Nasser entered the Egyptian Military Academy.

Meanwhile, with trouble in Iraq, Syria, Lebanon, and Egypt tying up British forces, Prime Minister Winston Churchill decided that some concessions must be made to Arab nationalism. Accordingly, after Farouk's collapse in February 1942 British Foreign Secretary Anthony Eden declared that His Majesty's government in London would support the cause of Arab unity. After prolonged and agonizingly intricate negotiations representatives of Egypt, Syria, Iraq, Lebanon, Trans-Jordan, Saudi Arabia, Yemen, and Palestinian Arabs met in Alexandria during September and October 1944. There they founded a loose Arab confederation to be known as the Arab League, which came formally into existence on March 22, 1945. The aims of the league remained rather vague; and if it seemed to herald a new age of Arab brotherhood, it was also an organization under British tutelage—another means whereby Britain could influence events in the Arab world.

All of which was observed by Captain Gamal Abdel Nasser with a realistic eye. He had already decided while still at the military academy that only through the army (the sole well-organized, disciplined institution in Egyptian society) could his country be redeemed—not only from the British, but also from its own decay. In pursuit of that goal Nasser and several fellow officers founded a secret revolutionary group within the army called the Free Officers' Association. They persuaded the prestigious Egyptian General Mohammed Neguib to become their titular chief and after the war ended in 1945 rapidly increased their membership. Then, with the establishment of the new Jewish state of Israel in Palestine in May 1948, came the first Arab-Israeli war, the roots and causes of which we will examine later.

From the Egyptian viewpoint this first Arab-Israeli conflict was an unmitigated disaster. The Egyptian government of King Farouk, reluctantly forced into the struggle by the pressure of the Moslem Brotherhood, proved itself utterly incapable of fighting a modern war. The Egyptian army officers, who watched their men die through government sloth, incompetence, cowardice, and corruption, joined the Free Officers' Association by the hundreds. Both General Neguib and Major Nasser were badly wounded during the fighting, which by January 1949 had all but destroyed the defeated Egyptian army.

The defeat in Palestine weakened the Moslem Brotherhood's hold on the Egyptian masses, but this was soon restored by renewed political agitation and terrorism against the British. King Farouk's government, if it was to maintain any sort of credibility and control over the country, had to curry popularity among those same masses by also pitting itself against its British patrons. And this led to disaster.

Since the end of the war in 1945 British troops in Egypt (some eighty thousand of them) had been withdrawn from the cities to be stationed in military bases along the British-owned and -operated Suez Canal. In October 1951, under irresistible public pressure, Farouk's government denounced the 1936 treaty and cut off all supplies to the British camps, which now became the targets of Moslem Brotherhood "liberation squads." With Egyptian police connivance these squads carried out increasingly bold, increasingly bloody sabotage operations and guerrilla raids against the British garrisons along the canal. Finally provoked beyond endurance, the British responded on January 25, 1952 (still known to Egyptians as Black Saturday) by surrounding Egyptian police headquarters in the canal city of Ismailia and ordering its immediate surrender. The police refused, and in the subsequent British assault fifty of them were killed. The next day huge mobs roamed the streets of Cairo and Alexandria attacking British property and civilians.

The Free Officers' Association decided the time had

come to intervene. They laid careful plans and in July 1952 swiftly, efficiently, and almost bloodlessly seized control of the Egyptian government. King Farouk was permitted to flee the country on his yacht, along with his mistresses and that part of his fortune which had not already been transferred to Swiss banks, to spend his declining years in the nightclubs and casinos of the French Riviera; but certain of his ministers were put on trial for their crimes against the Egyptian people. Both the monarchy and its parliamentary window dressing were abolished; and a new governing body, the Revolutionary Command Council, was formed as a military dictatorship, nominally headed by General Neguib but really controlled by Colonel Gamal Abdel Nasser with the help of Major Anwar Sadat. In all of this, as Nasser and his fellow Free Officers had foreseen, the British did not intervene. Farouk had become too unpopular to serve their interests any longer—and besides, a strong new Egyptian government might well be better able to control its own people and hence provide security against Moslem Brotherhood attacks.

To the Egyptian people the revolution of 1952 meant that at long last they were truly independent. Of course the British bases remained; but for the first time in two thousand years Egypt was now ruled by native Egyptians who would not accept domination or "tutelage" from any foreign source. This triumph of Arab nationalism in the strongest nation of the Near East was a twentieth-century turning point. Its repercussions were felt everywhere: in the already independent states of Syria, Lebanon, and Iraq; in neighboring Libya (which had been granted independence by the United Nations in 1946 as a result of Italy's defeat in World War II); in those Arab countries where British "advisors" still retained influence, such as Trans-Jordan, Saudi Arabia, Yemen, and the petty sheikhdoms of the Persian Gulf coast—but most especially in the remaining French colonies of western North Africa.

During the war these colonies had been invaded by Anglo-American forces. Displacing local Vichy authorities with Free French administrators, the Allies had used Morocco, Algeria, and Tunisia as important bases and staging areas for their invasion of southern Europe. After the war, with the departure of the Allied armies, the newly established government of the French Fourth Republic reasserted its control of the entire area. But French military power had suffered an irretrievable loss of prestige during the Second World War—and Arab nationalism had long been brewing in these provinces.

In Morocco Arab nationalists were organized into the Istiqlal (Independence) Party, which rallied its hopes behind the vigorous Sultan Mohammed V. French authorities in Morocco, supported by a French army of occupation under the command of tough General Juin (himself the son of a French Algerian family), attempted to pressure Mohammed V to dissociate himself from Istiqlal activities, but failed. During the early 1950s the Istiqlal movement spread from the cities of Fez, Rabat, and Casablanca to the Berber tribesmen of the hinterlands and mountains. The Moroccan nationalists had the support not only of the Arab League and the Afro-Asian members of the United Nations but also of a considerable body of French public opinion. For in France ordinary citizens had grown weary of paying taxes to support an imperialistic policy that benefited only a handful of companies and individuals with overseas investments.

But those companies and individuals, being wealthy, wielded great influence in Paris. So too did the French military, who, still smarting from their defeat by the Germans in World War II, determined not to retreat again anywhere. And these influential French voices were amplified by the vociferous support of a large population of French *colons* (colonists) in North Africa whose continued prosperity depended upon their uniquely exploitive position there. Bowing to these pressure groups, the French government in 1953 deposed Mohammed V and bundled him off to exile on the French island colony of Madagascar. He was replaced by his elderly (and subservient) cousin, Sidi ben Arafa.

But this outrageous action ignited full-scale rebellion and guerrilla warfare against the French throughout Morocco. General Juin took severe measures of reprisal; but French opinion at home would not condone the only measure that might have proven effective—wholesale massacre of the rebel populace. By 1955 matters had degenerated to the point where the desperate French could only restore peace by returning Mohammed V to his throne. This they did, and in November 1955 they agreed to end their mandate over the country. Since without French military protection Spain could not hope to maintain control of its small zone of occupation, the Spanish government also agreed to withdraw its forces. The arrangements were completed on March 2, 1956, and Morocco regained its complete independence. The pattern of events in Morocco was soon to be repeated in the rest of French North Africa.

In Tunisia the struggle against the French had begun as early as 1934, when a dynamic nationalist party, the Neo-Destour (New Constitution), was formed by a young Tunisian teacher named Habib Bourguiba. By 1938 the Destour organization had become sufficiently annoying to French authorities that it was harshly suppressed, Bourguiba himself going to prison. There he remained until he was freed by the German Army in 1942. Since it was Anglo-American policy to keep Arab nationalists calm behind the fighting lines, Bourguiba was not again imprisoned when Allied armies drove out the Germans later that same year. After the war the French attempted to woo the Tunisian nationalists through a more liberal policy. The Neo-

Destour was permitted to operate freely, as were certain other political parties. But the powerful French *colons* of Tunisia (they numbered some 180,000) would accept no weakening of French control. They prevailed upon the French government to again suppress any and all Tunisian independence movements and to imprison Habib Bourguiba again in 1951.

The harsh new policy led to the usual results: growing agitation, street demonstrations, bombings, murders, terrorism, and finally guerrilla warfare in the countryside. This in turn led to the usual French retaliations, until French terrorism matched Tunisian in ferocity and casualties mounted into the thousands on both sides. Again, French opinion at home was badly shaken by these events; and finally, in June 1954, a new French government headed by Premier Pierre Mendès-France agreed to recognize Tunisian autonomy within the French Union (as the diminishing French Empire was now hopefully called). Bourguiba was released from jail and became premier of a new Tunisian government staffed largely by members of his Neo-Destour Party. Despite the opposition of local *colons* the new Franco-Tunisian Convention formalizing these arrangements was signed in June 1955. This convention attempted to maintain certain French privileges in Tunisia, especially commercial privileges, and assumed continued French "protection" and sovereignty over the new autonomous state. But after continued Tunisian rioting all of this was swept aside by a new agreement in March 1956. Tunisia became fully independent and Habib Bourguiba was elected president as well as premier of the new nation.

Now France's willingness to concede independence to Morocco and Tunisia was partly motivated by its desire to conserve its forces in order to maintain control of the oldest, richest, and most important of all French colonies, Algeria. There were more than one million French *colons* in that huge country, and the families of many had been there for a century. They considered

Algeria their homeland and would hear of no relaxation of French authority. Indeed, over the years various French governments had advanced proposals to make Algeria a *département* of metropolitan France. Several formulas were worked out that provided for full French citizenship for Algeria's Arab populaton and even for Algerian representation in the French parliament on an equal per capita basis. But the induction of one hundred Moslem representatives into the *Chambre des Deputés* (the French lower house) was something that no French political party could contemplate; and so France was never able to offer Algerian Arabs anything more than a kind of tenth-class citizenship—and even this was bitterly opposed by the *colons*.

But French schemes to maintain control of Algeria were doomed to failure. There, as in the rest of North Africa, the tide of Arab natonalism was rising. The usual degeneration from protest through terrorism to guerrilla warfare took place between 1952 and 1956—by which year a full-scale rebellion had broken out. Led by a young socialist named Ahmed Ben Bella and Colonel Houari Boumedienne, the rebels formed an Algerian People's Liberation Army which maintained its hold on the deserts and mountains south of the coastal cities.

Fighting in Algeria was prolonged, savage, and devastating; it went on for six years, during which a French army of half a million men employed every measure to maintain control, from the torture of prisoners under interrogation to the forcible resettlement of more than a million Arab villagers. The seemingly endless war toppled the Fourth Republic itself. In May 1958, suspecting that the government in Paris was about to recognize Algerian independence, the intransigent Algerian *colons* combined forces with French rightist parties to bring General Charles de Gaulle back to power. Supposing that de Gaulle would never retreat from Algeria, the *colons* vigorously supported the new French constitution he promulgated, which concentrated powers in his own hands as president.

But the *colons* had mistaken their man. De Gaulle was, despite his romantic oratory, a realist. He had already concluded that France must withdraw from Algeria, and in the years following his resumption of power he moved slowly but decisively to achieve that objective. In 1960 and 1961 de Gaulle's now obvious "deception" caused the *colons,* in alliance with some army battalions, to come out in open revolt against the French government. But these uprisings were subdued by loyal French regiments. Despite this fiery opposition, and despite several assassination attempts against de Gaulle carried out by the *colon* Secret Army Organization, his policy remained inflexible. During 1961 he reached an understanding with the Algerian leaders, headed by Ben Bella, who had been released from a French prison to exile in Switzerland. Known as the Evian Agreements, this secret accord provided for the withdrawal of French troops from Algeria and the holding of a nationwide plebiscite there on the question of independence. When word of the Evian Agreements leaked out, the French *colons* panicked—more than eight hundred thousand of them fled Algeria precipitously, thereby solving one problem at a single stroke.

On July 1, 1962, Algerians voted overwhelmingly for full independence. Ahmed Ben Bella became the first premier of the new Algerian Republic in September of that same year. Over 130 years of French rule in North Africa had come to an end, and from the Persian Gulf to the Atlantic Ocean Islam was once again free. More than that, for the first time in twenty centuries native Arabs were masters of the Arab world.

But if we are to understand what uses the Arabs made of their hard-won independence, we must realize that their opportunities, their domestic policies, and their very freedom were contingent upon a complex international situation. From the Arab viewpoint that situation revolved around an ancient, vexing, bloody issue—the struggle for Palestine. Only in the light of that struggle can we comprehend the history of the Arab world since independence, and to it we now must turn.

CHAPTER NINE

Tragedy in the Promised Land

In the Name of God, the Compassionate, the Merciful
Make mention also in the Book, of Abraham;
for he was a man of truth, a Prophet.

KORAN, XIV

Now the Lord said unto Abraham, Get thee out of thy
country...unto the land that I will show thee:
and I will make of thee a great nation.

GENESIS 12:1

On the word of God himself Palestine is a country "flowing with milk and honey." It is a Holy Land, rich with
the dust of kings and prophets and saviors and miracles
sacred to three great religions. There on Mount Zion
Solomon built his temple and King David sang his
psalms; in its fragrant vineyards and olive groves Jesus
of Nazareth walked among men before and after his
crucifixion; to its golden capital, Jerusalem, Mohammed was wafted one night by the Archangel Gabriel that he might ascend from there to visit paradise.
Yet it has never been a land of peace; since before the
dawn of history men have battled for its possession.

In ancient times the land was known as Canaan, an
old Aramaic word meaning "purple," because its inhabitants were famous for their trade in purple dyes.
But in Greek the word for purple was *phonix*, and so
they called the country Phoenicia and its inhabitants
Phoenicians. The ancient Hebrews, however, rendered

Phoenicians into *Pelishtim* (Philistines), and later the Greek historian Herodotus wrote that word as *Palaistine*. Palestine it has remained to this day.

The land was already rich and well populated when the patriarch Abraham, obeying God's command, led his desert kinsmen east from Ur of the Chaldees to settle along the banks of the River Jordan. There ensued generations of conflict until Abraham's descendants had finally conquered the entire country. But Palestine was on the principal north-south trading route of the Near East, and control of that route was essential to the prosperity of the ancient empires. So Palestine was never long free from foreign domination—Egyptian, Assyrian, Babylonian, or Greek; and its inhabitants (who called themselves Israelites, after Abraham's grandson Jacob won the name Israel in a wrestling match with an angel) were often carried off into slavery or exile. Around the year 1300 B.C. they were held for nearly a century in Egypt, where they merged with the lowest caste of workers, known as *Hebiri* (Hebrews). But they escaped from the "House of Pharoah," led by the prophet Moses back to Palestine, the land promised them by God. And later, when many Israelites were held captive in Babylon, they too eventually returned to the land of their fathers. And through all their trials and triumphs the Israelites maintained their identity as a people through strict adherence to their uniquely monotheistic religion, Judaism (derived, as in the word *Jew*, from the name of the ancient Israelite kingdom of Judah).

For more than two thousand years before the birth of Christ Palestine was the homeland of the Jews and Jerusalem the holy city of their religion. Then came the Romans with their world-conquering legions and their political religion of emperor worship. Just as Christ could not stomach the Roman world order, neither could Jewish traditionalists. But while Jesus preached peace, most of his fellow countrymen undertook armed rebellion against Rome. There were upris-

ings and massacres, which culminated finally in A.D.
135 when the exasperated Romans finally destroyed
Jerusalem and drove most of Palestine's Jews into slavery or exile.

But not all of them. For there were Jews in Palestine
in A.D. 638, when Caliph Omar, second successor to
Mohammed, conquered the land for Islam. As we have
seen, Jews, like Christians, were well tolerated in the
pluralistic early Arab Empire. Except for repressions
brought about in various places by fanatical Islamic
puritan sects such as the Almohades (who in any case
repressed irreligious Moslems as severely as Jews and
Christians), Jews dispersed throughout the world of
Islam were free to practice their religion, to prosper,
and to achieve what it was in them to achieve. Such
unfortunately was not the case with Jews dispersed
throughout Christendom. For under the rule of Catholic Europeans (despite papal intercessions and orders
to the contrary) Jews endured nearly two thousand
years of persecution, deportations, segregation, and
wholesale massacre. When Caliph Omar entered Jerusalem, he left its Jews unmolested; when the Crusaders entered the Holy City five centuries later, they
murdered all the Jews (and Moslems) they could find.
True, the fanaticism and intolerance generated by the
thousand-year struggle between Islam and Christendom did sometimes spill over into Moslem persecution
of Jewish as well as Christian infidels. But by and
large, at least until the middle of the nineteenth century, Jews who lived in the Arab world might count
themselves much luckier than Jews who lived elsewhere.

But wherever they lived, Jews stubbornly clung to
their identity through their religion and dreamed of
the day they would once again create a nation of their
own in Palestine. For the love of Palestine was the very
core of Judaism; it was obedience to the express promise
and order of God, who through all the generations of
the Old Testament had commanded his people to live

in that land. Thus to be a religious Jew was also inescapably to be a Zionist—one who longed to repossess his ancient homeland and build again the temple on Mount Zion.

But the modern Zionist movement grew not so much from religious yearning as from harsh social and political necessity. For despite the "Enlightenment," despite the American, French, and Industrial revolutions, despite the emergence of democratic societies, by the middle of the nineteenth century Jews remained at best unwelcome guests in Christian Europe. And as the "century of progress" wore on, things got worse, not better. The 1880s saw terrible massacres of Jews in Czarist Russia and Poland and the flight of hundreds of thousands to refuge in the United States. But even in Western Europe anti-Semitism—a political tool of unscrupulous politicians, made supposedly respectable by new, perverted, "scientific" racist theories—was on the rise, throwing threatening shadows on the future.

It seemed to many Jews that only by building a nation they could call their own could they finally escape Christian persecution. And to build that nation anywhere in the world but Palestine was unthinkable. As early as 1882 Russian Jews, organized into small *Chovevei Zion* (Lovers of Zion) societies, began sending small groups of "pioneers" to Palestine to lay the foundations for a new nation. These and later settlers bought land from local Arabs or Turks and labored to bring it under cultivation. There were already some twenty-five thousand Jews living in Palestine upon their arrival; the new settlers were to double that population by 1914. Then in 1896 an Austrian-Jewish journalist and playwright named Theodore Herzl, who had been shocked and alarmed by the anti-Semitic frenzy that swept France after a Jewish captain on the French General Staff named Alfred Dreyfus was falsely convicted of treason, published a short book called *Der Judenstaat (The Jewish State)*. In it he developed the rationale and the method by which a new Jewish nation might be born in Palestine. "Jews who will it," wrote Herzl, "shall have a state of their own."

Herzl did more than write; he devoted the rest of his life to organizing Jews throughout the world into Zionist Congresses which met every other year in various European cities, begging funds from such wealthy Jews as the Rothschild banking family and pleading the case for a Jewish Palestine before politicians and heads of state—including (since Palestine was then part of Turkish-ruled Syria) the Ottoman Sultan Abdul Hamid. At first scoffed at as a wild, romantic dream, Zionism soon gained the support of Jews everywhere and of many Christians too, especially in France, England, and the United States. Herzl died in 1904, his vision still unrealized; but by that time the well-organized World Zionist Movement had become a real force in international politics. It patronized increased Jewish emigration to the Holy Land and also organized and administered Jewish settlements there—with the usually inefficient "cooperation" of Ottoman authorities, who hoped Jewish enterprise in Palestine would increase the area's taxable wealth. Then, when the Ottoman Empire went to war against the Allies in 1914, such Zionist leaders as the British-Russian chemist Chaim Weizmann and the American Supreme Court Justice Louis D. Brandeis saw an opportunity. Since Britain and France were planning the dismemberment of the Ottoman domains anyhow, why not reserve Palestine for the Jews? Great Britain, close to defeat in 1917 and eager for the support of Zionists throughout the world, responded to their pleas with the Balfour Declaration.

This declaration spoke of the establishment of a "national home" for Jews "*in* Palestine" and carefully protected the "existing rights" of the area's other inhabitants—meaning Palestinian Arabs. Nonetheless, while Zionists rejoiced, Arabs grew first alarmed and then wrathful. Arab nationalism, aroused by Britain as a weapon against the Turks, demanded an independent Arab kingdom of Palestine. Their hopes shattered and betrayed at the Paris Peace Conference, Arabs fought the British mandate established over Palestine just as they fought the mandate system elsewhere in the Near East. But the struggle against the British in Palestine became particularly venomous because the Arabs were convinced that the British intended eventually to turn it into a Jewish nation. The rapid rise of Jewish immigration into the Holy Land in the years between the wars (there were more than 450,000 Jews there by 1939) and their creation of new industries, new farming communities, and new cities such as Tel Aviv, seemed to presage a total Jewish takeover. Arab nationalist riots and terrorism, which during the early years of the mandate were directed primarily against British occupation authorities, soon turned into violent attacks against Palestine's Jewish communities. In response (and because the British afforded little protection) the Jews organized self-defense forces such as the Haganah (of which David Ben-Gurion and Moshe Dayan were both members) and the more aggressive Irgun-zvi-Leumi (led for a while by Menachem Begin). Despite British pronouncements promising all things to all men Palestine during the 1930s slid into almost full-scale civil war between Jews and Arabs. The British were unable to control either and only by promising to tightly restrict future Jewish immigration and abandon the idea of a Jewish national home in Palestine could they impose some semblance of peace and order upon that strategically vital area when World War II broke out.

Then, during the war years, without the effective opposition of any single nation anywhere in the world, came Hitler's holocaust, during which more than six million European Jews—men, women, and children— were murdered in the Nazi death factories. Their isolation and helplessness in the face of this unutterably frightful crime left upon the minds of Jews everywhere a scar that may never be healed. The Jews of Palestine (fifty thousand of whom fought with the Allies during the war) and Zionists throughout the world became doubly convinced that only in a nation of their own could Jews find ultimate peace, dignity, and simple survival. The fact that such a nation could only be founded in Palestine was an imperative of Jewish history; that Palestine should also be the homeland of more than a million Arabs was a fact of Islamic history.

The British tried at the war's end to continue their juggling act in Palestine just as they did elsewhere in the Near East. They sought to pacify the Arabs by forbidding the entrance into Palestine of that pitiful handful of Jewish refugees from Europe who had survived the holocaust. The Royal Navy patrolled the Palestinian coast to intercept Jewish refugee vessels, but the Haganah and the Irgun smuggled many past the British blockade anyhow. And world opinion, in Russia, the United States, and England itself (where Churchill described the Labour Party's Near Eastern policy as "this ignominious and squalid war against the Jews"), demanded Britain's withdrawal and the creation in one form or another of a Jewish state in Palestine. So under pressure from the United Nations and a barrage of Haganah and Irgun terrorist attacks the British departed. On May 14, 1948, David Ben-Gurion, in a solemn ceremony at Tel Aviv, announced the establishment of the new nation of Israel. The next day, May 15, the British mandate over Palestine came to its inglorious end; and one minute after midnight on May 16 the armies of Syria, Trans-Jordan, and Egypt attacked the new state.

The United Nations had sought desperately to avoid this tragedy; innumerable experts, study groups, commissions, and committees had offered possible "peaceful solutions" to the problem. They ranged all the way from a federated Jewish-Arab Republic to the partition of Palestine between Jews and Arabs, and they all had one thing in common: they were always unacceptable. So too with the final United Nations Plan adopted by the General Assembly in October 1947. It proposed partition of the Holy Land, with the Arabs (who composed about two thirds of the population and owned 46 percent of the land) retaining almost everything they already had and the Jews (who were now one third of the population but owned only 6 percent of the land) receiving the rest. Which meant that the Jews were to be awarded primarily control over land (mainly in the arid Negev desert) not presently occupied by anyone else. Jerusalem was to come under the authority of a UN commission which would administer the city in the name of humanity. The Jews announced their acceptance of this plan—but the Arabs rejected it entirely. Why?

Palestinian Arabs were opposed because they frankly feared that Jewish energy, money, technology, and expertise would soon swallow them up or displace them no matter how Palestine might be divided. Religious Arabs everywhere were hostile to the idea that their sacred places in Jerusalem might pass under foreign control. The Syrian government hoped to reestablish its own control over Palestine, a Syrian province until 1918. King Abdullah of Trans-Jordan hoped to seize the Holy Land for himself, since that would afford his landlocked country a seaport.

But basic to all other reasons was the dangerous fact that the vast masses of Arabs everywhere, from Casablanca to Baghdad, vociferously demanded the expulsion of the Jews from Palestine. It was this explosive popular pressure from below that forced the leaders of such nations as Egypt, Iraq, and Saudi Arabia—countries with no apparent direct stake in the outcome—to join in the war against Israel. Yet widespread anti-Jewish xenophobia was something new in Islam—it had developed only since 1919. It was not at first anti-Jewish per se (Jews living in Arab lands beyond Palestine remained unmolested before 1948); but with Arab defeats in battle it soon became so. It was a sentiment so unworthy of and so totally contrary to the

ancient Arab traditions of tolerance and pluralism that
it demands explanation.

The *jihad* against a Jewish state in Palestine grew
out of the frustrations and bitterness of long-sup-
pressed Arab nationalism which, once inflamed, fed
upon itself. Struggling to rid themselves of foreign
domination, Arabs in other lands saw the Jewish presence in the Near East as simply the latest and most
outrageous intrusion of European imperialism upon
Islam. Indeed, many Arab nationalist leaders used the
plight of Palestinian Arabs to whip up independence
movements at home. Then too the fight against a common enemy seemed to offer a rallying point for the
cause of Arab unity. After all, in the days of their greatness Arabs had been one nation; only foreign intervention had shattered the wholeness of Islam—the war
against Israel might restore it. Unable during the late
1940s to strike directly against their colonial masters,
Arabs struck out against the eternal scapegoat, the
Jews—and were in fact encouraged to do so by certain
of those same imperial masters, who shortsightedly
hoped to divert Arab nationalism from its proper targets. In short, at the end of World War II Arabs everywhere were passionately determined to once more rule
their own world—and for nearly fifteen centuries Palestine had been part of that world.

The armed battle had begun even before the British
withdrawal, as Syrian and Iraqi "volunteers," calling
themselves the Palestine Army of National Liberation
(though very few Palestinians were to be found in their
ranks), carried on heavy guerrilla warfare against Jewish communities in Israel. These irregular forces were
joined by the armies of Egypt, Syria, and Trans-Jordan
in May 1948. The ensuing fight was bitter, prolonged,
costly, and eventually disastrous for the Arabs. Although the British-trained Trans-Jordanian Legion
was able to seize control of the West Bank of the Jordan
River and of the Old City of Jerusalem, the Israelis
prevailed everywhere else in the Holy Land. In the end

the Jews had won slightly *more* room in Palestine (including the New City of Jerusalem) than had been awarded them by the UN in the first place. But although the beaten Arabs agreed to a truce in October 1948, they would make no peace with a nation whose very existence they refused to recognize.

One unique feature of this first war of Israeli independence was the departure from Palestine of hundreds of thousands of native Arabs. In some cases they simply fled the fighting, in some cases they were driven out by the Jews. But the great majority of them left at the orders of the Arab High Command, which wanted, they claimed, a clear field of fire against the enemy. Thus, for example, when the Haganah entered Jaffa—although no fighting had taken place there, and despite the fact that the Israelis had declared that they had no intention of incorporating the city in their new state—they found it a ghost town, its hundred thousand Arab residents gone. This mass flight of Palestinian Arabs from their homeland, provoked mainly by the fiery propaganda of Arab League orators, was the tragic beginning of that Palestinian refugee problem which has plagued the Near East ever since.

As we have seen, the Arab defeat in 1948 led directly a few years later to the overthrow of King Farouk in Egypt, but its consequences were felt more immediately in Syria and Trans-Jordan. In Syria defeat led to the imposition of a military dictatorship that during the early 1950s was to sweep away almost all the democratic and parliamentary formal institutions inherited from the days of the French mandate. In Trans-Jordan it led the Emir Abdullah to throw off the last vestiges of British tutelage and proclaim himself ruler of the new Kingdom of Jordan in 1948. Thereafter the newly elevated king devoted himself to the construction of a summer palace on conquered Palestinian land near Jerusalem.

Now if one thing had been made clear to the Arabs by the disaster in Palestine, it was that only through

unity could they hope to defeat the Israelis—and furthermore, that only Egypt had the strength to lead a
unified Arab community in the Near East. But although Gamal Abdel Nasser and the other Free Officers who ruled Egypt after the 1952 revolution cherished this ambition, they wisely decided to put first
things first. And first of all on their program was the
final elimination of British forces and influence from
Egypt and the Anglo-Egyptian Sudan.

Nasser tackled the Sudanese problem first. In 1953
he succeeded in winning a treaty from Britain whereby
both Egyptian and British authority in the Sudan
would be terminated by free elections in which the
Sudanese people would decide their own future. No
doubt both sides hoped that these elections would pro-
duce a Sudanese regime favorable to themselves. Both
were disappointed: the newly elected Sudanese government proclaimed the full independence of their nation on January 1, 1956.

With the Sudan problem settled, Nasser turned next
to the question of the British bases along the Suez
Canal and the eighty thousand British troops still stationed there. Negotiations were long and bitter; it was
hard for the British to accept the fact that their days
of imperial glory were coming to an end. But since
Englishmen at home were neither willing nor able to
continue paying the price in treasure and blood to
maintain their empire, British negotiators were forced
to concede. In July 1955 they agreed upon the withdrawal of British troops, and by March 31, 1956, the
last of these troops had departed from Egyptian soil.
The Suez Canal itself, however, was still to be administered by the British-dominated international company that owned it. But Egypt had not seen the last
of the British.

For by the mid-1950s international politics in the
Near East and throughout the Arab world were becoming ever more deeply embroiled in that prolonged West-
ern-Soviet confrontation known as the Cold War. Both

sides in that struggle were well aware of the strategic importance of the Near East, and both tried to gain influence in the area.

Nasser and other Arab leaders strove to maintain neutrality. They were traditionally opposed to atheistic communism and deeply suspicious of Russian motives. On the other hand they wanted no part of American Secretary of State John Foster Dulles's anticommunist crusade. Instead they looked forward to an independent bloc of Arab states allied to other neutral third world nations. But these same leaders were faced with two decisive problems. First, they had to rapidly lift the masses of their own people from the harsh poverty they had so long endured, and secondly, they had to supply their armies with new weapons and training in order to confront the Israelis. If they failed in either of these tasks, they would face revolution at home. But to resolve both problems they required outside money and technology. Where would they get that vital assistance, from Russia or the West? And what price would they have to pay for it?

Nasser turned first to the United States. The new Egyptian government cherished a plan whereby it would construct a dam across the Nile River at Aswan. This would help both to irrigate millions of new acres of farmland and to generate electricity. It was to be the cornerstone of Egypt's plan for industrialization and self-sufficiency. But Nasser's refusal to align himself with the West against Russia led the United States and Britain to reject his pleas for financial and technical aid. Nasser's response was to announce on July 26, 1956, the Egyptian nationalization of the Suez Canal. Henceforth it would be run and managed by Egyptians and its revenues added to the impoverished Egyptian economy instead of lining the pockets of European shareholders in Paris and London.

Now if the British hated Nasser (who had somehow become a symbol of their loss of empire everywhere), the French had no liking for him either. The Egyptian

leader publicly supported the cause of Arab independence in French Algeria and, as the French supposed,
secretly aided the rebels there with money and supplies. The two powers determined to topple this upstart
Arab and cast about for an excuse and means to do so.

They found both in the continuing Arab-Israeli conflict. For ever since 1949, although there had been no
full-scale war, the Arabs had maintained an economic
blockade of Israel and had been carrying on guerrilla
and terrorist attacks against the new state. The Israelis
responded by bombing the guerrilla bases in Syria and,
late in 1955, Egyptian army headquarters in Gaza.
These raids and counterraids grew more intense during
1956. On October 24 of that year Britain, France, and
Israel reached a secret agreement to join forces in an
attempt to topple Nasser's Egyptian government.

Five days later Israel invaded Egypt across the Suez
Canal. Britain and France immediately issued an ultimatum to both sides to cease fighting and withdraw
their respective armies ten miles from the canal—
which, the two powers proclaimed, must be protected
in the interests of the entire world. The Israelis, whose
forces were not yet up to the ten-mile limit, gladly
accepted the ultimatum; Nasser, who would have to
withdraw his army from Egypt's own territory, rejected
it.

Accordingly, on October 31 British and French
planes bombed Egyptian airfields and on November 5
landed an Anglo-French army at Port Said. But the
days of such imperialistic interventions were long past,
although this was not yet fully appreciated in Paris
and London. Appreciation came swiftly when the Soviet government of Nikita Khrushchev publicly threatened massive Russian intervention on behalf of Egypt
and the American government of Dwight D. Eisen-
hower (which had been kept in the dark about the entire matter) angrily demanded immediate Anglo-French
withdrawal. So under intense international pressure
Britain and France sulkingly abandoned their enter-

prise, and the Israeli armies returned to their homeland. The only nation involved in this shabby business
to emerge from it with enhanced prestige was the intended victim, Egypt. Her leader, Gamal Abdel Nasser,
was now enshrined throughout the Arab world as the
heroic champion of Islam.

Angry Arab reaction to the Suez affair brought radical new leaders to power in both Syria and Iraq during
1957 and 1958. It led too to the linking of Syria and
Egypt under Nasser's leadership in the United Arab
Republic established in February 1958. It brought
about popular uprisings in Lebanon (quelled by U.S.
marines) and Jordan (whose King Abdullah had been
assassinated in 1951 and which was now ruled by his
grandson, King Hussein), which were put down by British paratroopers. It was only necessary for Arab nationalists to accuse the Saudi Arabian royal family of
plotting against Nasser to bring about the replacement
of King Saud by his brother, Faisal, in March 1958.
Everywhere Arabs turned to new and, in most cases,
more violent anti-Western leadership.

The Soviet Union was not slow to take advantage
of the situation. She had already agreed to help Egypt
build the Aswan Dam and had begun resupplying and
retraining the Egyptian army. Now Soviet arms, advisors, and technicians also appeared in Syria and Iraq.
But this very increase of Russian influence soon began
to strain the structure of Arab unity.

The governments of Saudi Arabia and Jordan were,
after all, traditionalist monarchies; the government of
Lebanon was a delicate balancing act between Christian and Moslem businessmen. All three feared Soviet
penetration of the Near East as a threat to their domestic stability. And despite radical leadership so too
did many segments of the Syrian, Iraqi, and Egyptian
populations. There were, for example, powerful religious organizations in all those countries that deplored
the spread of "materialistic" ideas; there were merchants and bankers who feared for their investments;

there were military men whose views remained essentially conservative despite the bright new weapons given them by Russian technicians; and, most important of all, there was a continuing impulse among all Arabs toward national independence and fulfillment—which meant that they did not intend to replace Western domination with a new Soviet tutelage.

Underlying all international problems, however, remained the central domestic problem: how to modernize Arab society, to alleviate the poverty afflicting its masses, develop responsive governmental institutions, and yet preserve what was best and vital in the deeply rooted religious traditions of Islam.

In the years after 1958 Nasser addressed himself to this urgent matter. His plans to rebuild Egyptian society progressed fitfully, slowly. It was soon apparent that Egypt simply did not possess sufficient private resources to advance along the road of capitalism. This led to the nationalization of more and more commercial and industrial sectors of the economy until by the mid-1960s something called "Arab socialism" had emerged. This was not, however, theoretical Marxism in action, nor was it a copy of Soviet institutions. Instead it was a haphazard, pragmatic emergency response to various economic crises as they developed. But it was sufficiently frightening to more conservative elements in Syria to cause Syrian withdrawal from the United Arab Republic in 1961. By this time, in any case, the burden of trying to govern Syria *and* Egypt had become an intolerable strain; Nasser did nothing to prevent the separation.

In a sense, after 1958 Gamal Nasser was a captive of his own image. The Arab masses had all but deified him and expected him to show them the path of domestic reform as well as to lead them one day to triumph over the Israelis. This latter confrontation was something Nasser did not want. He was too well aware of continued Arab military weakness, despite Soviet aid and training. But there was now a new and explosive factor in Arab affairs.

This factor was the growth of self-conscious nationalism among the Palestinian Arab refugees. After the Arab defeat in 1948 there were two possible solutions to the refugee problem caused by the flight of hundreds of thousands of Arabs from Palestine to neighboring countries: they could either return to their native land or be absorbed into the societies of their host nations. But the refugees refused to return to a land now ruled by Jews—nor were the Israelis anxious to have them back. Besides, Arab orators kept assuring them that it would be only a matter of months, perhaps a year or two, before Israel was wiped out and its Jews driven into the sea; then they could go home in triumph.

The second solution, absorption into other Arab societies, also failed to materialize. Again, the Palestinians wanted to live in an Arab Palestine, not in Syria, Egypt, or Jordan. Nor were the lands to which they had fled prepared to accept them as citizens; for this, it was feared, would prove an intolerable strain on these lands' already weak economies. And there were some Arab leaders who intended that the Palestinians remain refugees for the anti-Israeli propaganda that could be squeezed from their plight.

So in the end, although some fortunate few were albe to find jobs and homes in Damascus, Amman, or Cairo, the vast majority of refugees lived in miserably squalid camps in Syria and Jordan, maintained and supported by the United Nations. Over the years their numbers naturally increased, and their deep and festering hatred of Israel and of all who supported Israel grew ever more bitter.

Up until 1965–1966 guerilla and terrorist attacks against Israel had been carried out largely by Syrian, Jordanian, or Egyptian irregular forces. But after that time the Palestinians themselves, organized into various terrorist groups, began to attack. The largest of these groups was al-Fatah (Victory), which issued its first communiqué on January 1, 1965, claiming "credit" for the sabotage of Israeli irrigation works along the Jordan River. Another was the Palestine Liberation Organization (PLO), which until 1967 was sponsored by the Egyptians, who were training a Palestine Liberation Army in Gaza. Yet another was the Popular Front for the Liberation of Palestine (PFLP), headquartered in Syria. We shall take a closer look at these organizations and their leaders later. For the moment it is important to underscore the fact that their ceaseless attacks on Israeli citizens and property grew to intolerable proportions between 1965 and 1967. And Israel did not hesitate to strike back with bombing raids against suspected terrorist bases—most of which were in Syria. During the spring of 1967 Israel issued increasingly severe warnings to the Syrian government regarding their support of commando raids. Arab (and Soviet) intelligence agencies warned Nasser that Israel was preparing to launch a surprise attack against Syria, still Egypt's closest ally even though it had withdrawn from the UAR in 1961.

Nasser's response, on May 18, 1967, was to demand that United Nations forces in the Sinai Desert (which had been stationed between Egyptian and Israeli armies ever since the Suez affair) be withdrawn. He then closed the Gulf of Aqaba to Israeli shipping by planting artillery at Sharm al-Sheikh at its mouth. Why, it may be asked, did Nasser, who for eleven years had avoided war, take these aggressive steps? Simply because if he had not, he might well have been overthrown by his own military leaders. The entire Arab world was in a fever of anti-Israeli feeling, and this self-intoxicating emotional tide could not be stemmed even by the most realistic politicians.

Certain that the Arabs meant war, on June 5, 1967, the Israelis made a surprise attack on seventeen Egyptian airfields, thereby destroying almost all the Egyptian air force on the ground. This was followed by a lightning drive by Israeli armored forces, which in just

four days drove the Egyptian army in total defeat back
to the west bank of the Suez Canal and occupied all of
the Sinai Peninsula. Since both Syria and Jordan had
entered the battle on Egypt's side as soon as the first
bombs started falling, the Israelis next turned on the
Jordanians, driving them entirely from the West Bank
region of the Jordan River and from the Old City of
Jerusalem, both of which areas they then occupied. At
the same time, other Israeli forces captured and held
the Syrian positions on the Golan Heights. The fighting
in this brilliant campaign lasted just six days before
all the belligerents accepted a UN demand for cease-
fire, which left the Israelis securely ensconced in their
conquered territories.

So shattering was the Arab defeat in the Six Day
War that it seemed certain that Gamal Nasser must
now fall from power. In fact he announced his intention
of resigning the Egyptian presidency over Cairo television on June 9, when Israeli forces reached the canal.
"Arab unity began before Nasser," he told his audience,
"and will remain after him. I always told you that it
is the nation that survives. . . . I am not liquidating the
revolution. But it is not the property of one generation."
But so firm was Nasser's place in Egyptian hearts that
he was simply not permitted to resign. The roars of
"Nasser, Nasser, Nasser" that reverberated through
the streets of Cairo and Alexandria were echoed in
distant Damascus, Beirut, and Baghdad.

Yet despite the unshakability of Nasser's personal
prestige throughout the Arab world, it was now apparent that Arab policy toward Israel could no longer
be grounded on the single emotion of hatred, which
meant ultimately that it must be disentangled from
that complex of feelings known as Arab nationalism.
Some Arabs might assure each other that just as the
Crusaders had eventually been expelled from the Near
East after three hundred years, so too the Jews would
be driven into the sea. But after June 1967 these boasts
rang ever more hollow in Arab ears. The anti-Israeli

focus of Arab nationalism had warped relations between the Arab nations and with the rest of the world; it had delayed and twisted much-needed domestic reform and economic progress. It had cost Arab governments not only military defeat and humiliation but also priceless time and energy. It was in short a detour and blind alley on the road to modernization and self-fulfillment. Despite the passions of their peoples, after 1967 Arab leaders would have to seek a new and more realistic path into the future.

CHAPTER TEN

Not Peace but a Sword

In the Name of God, the Compassionate, the Merciful
And we gave to the people who had been brought so low,
the eastern and the western lands...and the good
word of thy Lord was fulfilled on the children of
Israel because they had borne up with patience...

KORAN, VII

The first and most immediate result of the 1967 defeat
was not, however, an access of realism among some
Arabs, but rather a dramatic increase in the kind of
fruitless violence that had caused the debacle in the
first place. For after the crushing humiliation of the
Arab regular armies the leaders of the Palestinian refugees decided that only through their own terrorist
activities could they reconquer their homeland. To be
sure, they depended upon the generosity of outside individuals and Arab governments for arms and money,
but after the Six Day War they considered themselves
commanders of front-line forces.

The Egyptian-sponsored Palestinian Liberation Organization (PLO), led by a wordy Palestinian lawyer
named Ahmad Shukairy, had not performed well during the fighting around its training grounds in Gaza.
Indeed, Shukairy seemed to be a man of words only.
Not so Dr. George Habash, leader of the Popular Front

for the Liberation of Palestine (PFLP). A Christian Palestinian from Lydda, Habash had earned his medical degree from the American University of Beirut, Lebanon. He had founded his movement originally among Arab students and for several years had been content to place his hopes in Nasser's leadership of the Arab cause. But after 1967 he changed his mind. Henceforth he preached that the Palestinian struggle against Israel must be pursued by *every* possible means, including plane hijackings, sabotage, and bombings both inside *and outside* Israeli territory. Anything was justified that could be perceived as harmful to Israeli interests; and if wholly innocent men, women, and children were killed, well, that was sad but unavoidable.

But the most influential and elusive Palestinian leader to emerge after 1967 was undoubtedly Yasir Arafat, head of al-Fatah. Born in 1929, Arafat was the scion of a wealthy Palestinian Arab family. He studied in Egypt and while there joined the fanatical Moslem Brotherhood. From 1959 onward he devoted himself to organizing his own Palestinian movement, with headquarters in Cairo but branches in Lebanon, Iraq, Kuwait, and even Western Europe. It was in Kuwait (where Arafat owned an engineering company) that the first al-Fatah cell was formed. Later, links were established with the Arab government of Algeria, which provided al-Fatah with a recruiting center and training camps. But Algeria was too distant from the Near East to provide a proper military base; this was found in Syria, to which al-Fatah headquarters were moved just before the 1967 war. It was from Syria that al-Fatah terrorist raids into Israel helped bring about that war.

Shukairy, Habash, and Arafat (and leaders of smaller terrorist groups) met secretly in Cairo shortly after the Six Day War to discuss joint action. But they could not agree. A second meeting in Cairo, at a so-called Palestinian Congress in 1968, brought Arafat into leadership of the PLO, which now combined with al-Fatah—but Habash's more radical PFLP refused to accept any merger. On only one objective were all the Palestinian groups agreed—the total destruction of the state of Israel. As to what should then become of Israel's Jewish population was a matter left ominously vague by Arafat and Habash, though they announced their intention of creating a democratic, nonsectarian (i.e., pluralistic) Palestinian nation from which no one should be expelled and in which Christians, Jews, and Moslems would live in peace. But the savagery with which al-Fatah and PFLP terrorists attacked Israeli markets, schools, airports, overseas consulates, and airliners completely undermined any possible Jewish faith in Palestinian promises.

Meanwhile the growth of al-Fatah-PLO commando forces in Lebanon and Jordan, where they and their fellow Palestinian refugees formed a kind of state-within-a-state, posed an increasingly severe threat to the governments of those countries. The strain was aggravated by the fact that every time al-Fatah struck against Israel or its citizens, the Israelis responded with violent attacks on terrorist targets *within* Lebanon and Jordan. Although outright civil war in Lebanon between PLO forces and the Lebanese army was averted, such was not the case in Jordan. There King Hussein was determined to be master in his own house. Accordingly, in September 1970 (Black September to the guerrillas) the Jordanian army attacked PLO guerrilla bases there and after bitter fighting (which did not fully end until July 1971) utterly destroyed the Palestinian Liberation Movement in Jordan. But the PLO, the PFLP, and smaller terrorist groups (including one now called Black September) continued their activities from bases in Iraq and Syria.

Although the terrorist attacks were bloody and newsmaking, a more important campaign against Israel was waged from 1968 to 1970 along the Suez Canal front in Egypt. As soon as Israeli forces had reached the canal in 1967, the Egyptians had sunk ships to block passage of this vital world trade artery. Since that time, although unable to launch any full-scale attack on the Israelis, the Egyptians had waged a commando-raid war of attrition, costly to both sides. This Nasser was forced to do if he hoped to retain the loyalty of his military commanders. But the Egyptian president never ceased searching for a way out of his impossible no peace–no war situation. He thought he had found it in the plan offered by American Secretary of State William Rogers during the summer of 1970.

The Rogers Plan, put forward with the support of President Richard Nixon and his (then) National Security Council head, Dr. Henry Kissinger, was based on acceptance of United Nations Resolution 242. This was the resolution adopted by the Security Council in November 1967 that called for withdrawal of Israeli forces "from territories occupied in the recent conflict" and for the right of *all* Near Eastern states to "live in peace within secure and recognized boundaries." It will be noted that the resolution did not require Israel to withdraw from *all* occupied territory, but it did by inference include Israel among *all* Near Eastern states. The resolution was thus left purposely vague. Israel rejected it because she would hear of no withdrawal without final peace treaties growing out of direct, face-to-face negotiations with the Arab countries—nor had she any intention of withdrawing from Jerusalem, which after 1967 had become her capital. The Arabs rejected Resolution 242 because it implied recognition of the state of Israel. The Americans now proposed a cease-fire in the Egyptian-Israeli war of attrition, to be followed by Israeli withdrawal to her pre-1967 borders except for "insubstantial changes." Hoping that the United States could pressure Israel into acceptance, Nasser agreed to the cease-fire in August 1970.

But time was now running out for the Egyptian president. He had ruled his nation since 1952, and the strain of revolution, reform, and unending war had undermined his strength. In September 1970 he pre-

sided over an Arab summit meeting in Cairo which
tried unsuccessfully to end the fighting between the
PLO and the Jordanian army, but the effort was too
much; he suffered a heart attack on September 27 and
died a few hours later. When he was buried on October
1, 1970, tens of thousands of Egyptians followed his
coffin through the streets of Cairo amid scenes of un
paralleled grief. So ended the career of one of the key
figures of the twentieth century—a victim to forces he
himself had encouraged and led.

Even before his death, however, Nasser had indi
cated his choice of Anwar Sadat to be his successor
Sadat had been part of the Egyptian government ever
since the days of the 1952 revolution and the Revolu
tionary Command Council, but he had not been prom
inent, nor was he widely known. In recent years he had
been president of the Egyptian National Assembly; but
since the assembly was never more than a rubber
stamp for government policy, this had hardly taxed his
abilities. It was perhaps precisely because Sadat was
obscure and uncontroversial that Nassar appointed
him vice-president of Egypt in January 1970.

Anwar Sadat's inheritance was far from enviable
The no peace—no war situation with Israel persisted
and it became clearer daily that the United States had
no intention of forcing Israel into withdrawing from
the conquered territories. The cease-fire of 1967 had
mostly benefited the Israelis, who were apparently pre
pared to maintain themselves in the Sinai forever. So
cial and economic discontent among the Egyptian peo
ple was on the rise. And radical students as well as
aggressive military men were calling for yet another
all-out attack against Israel, an attack for which Sadat
knew Egypt to be wholly unprepared.

Quietly but firmly the new Egyptian president as
serted his control over the turbulent country. Ministers
and public officials who opposed his policies were re
placed and a general relaxation of Egyptian political
life followed. During Nasser's eighteen-year rule the
nation had become so used to what amounted to one-

man government (despite constitutional window dressing) that political reforms had to be introduced with great care lest they lead to anarchy. What Sadat promised his people was an eventual return to the rule of law, not men, and the reinvigoration of democratic institutions. Yet while Egypt suffered from poverty and underdevelopment, and especially so long as anti-Israeli belligerence had to be maintained, these objectives could not be attained. Without authoritarian rule Egyptian society simply could not withstand the continuing strains placed upon it. So after a few months Anwar Sadat found himself, like his predecessor, virtual dictator of Egypt, whether he wished to be or not.

Shrewdly assessing the situation at home and abroad, Anwar Sadat realized that he had but little time in which to solve the problems confronting him. For example, on the international scene the days of the Cold War were not past. Soviet-American détente was growing warmer, and this meant that it was becoming less and less possible for small nations to play the two superpowers off against each other. So when in June 1971 Sadat signed a fifteen-year treaty of friendship and cooperation with the Soviet Union (which undertook to re-equip Egypt's armed forces) he feared no reprisals from Washington. Indeed, American policy of unquestioning support for Israel and neglect of the Arab nations in the Near East seemed to be frozen. To change that policy became Sadat's overriding ambition. Therefore he reached decisions in 1971 which he kept entirely to himself while biding his time.

If we have concentrated in these pages on the development of Egypt, Syria, and Jordan—the so-called front line states in the anti-Israeli *jihad*—it is because so much of the Arab world's energies were poured into the struggle between 1948 and 1970. But these years saw important developments in all the Arab lands.

In Egypt's neighbor Libya, oil had been discovered in the mid-1950s. It was exploited by an Anglo-American company, whose royalty payments to Libya's aged

King Idris did little to change the poverty most Libyans suffered. But in September 1969 a group of young Libyan army officers headed by Colonel Muammar al-Qaddafy deposed the king (who was in Turkey for medical treatment at the time) and declared a republic. But unlike other Arab rebellions the one in Libya was not even partly motivated by left-wing political theory. It was in fact a highly conservative movement. Qaddafy and his fellow officers were puritanical Moslem fanatics much like the Almohades of old. Their republic speedily declined into a military dictatorship intent on rebuilding Libyan society according to the religious precepts of Islam. Thus drinking, gambling, and smoking were banned, women's rights were severely limited and education was dominated by study of the Koran. The Anglo-American oil enterprise was nationalized and Colonel Qaddafy emerged as the most extreme of all Arab nationalists. Enriched by her oil revenues Libya now became the patron of the Palestinian guerrilla movements, supplying them with money, arms and training camps. Colonel Qaddafy even boasted that he was supplying arms to underground movements in the United States and to the Irish Catholic rebels of Northern Ireland. So loudmouthed, ill-informed, and politically intransigent was this fervent Moslem puritan that he soon became a positive embarrassment to the Arab cause. During 1971 and 1972 Qaddafy undertook to merge his nation with Egypt; but after meeting him in Cairo (where the colonel did not hesitate to lecture a group of Egyptian ministers' wives, using a blackboard and chalk diagrams, on why women were permanently and inescapably inferior to men) President Sadat backed off the project.

In the Arab states of North Africa west of Libya change was perhaps not so dramatic, but it was more in line with twentieth-century realities. Tunisia, Libya's western neighbor, was for many years after it achieved independence in 1956 no more than a reflection of the amazing personality of its president, Habi

Bourguiba. A man who prided himself on his logic, Bourguiba was a constant critic of the emotional Arab nationalism that kept the Near East aflame. This lofty view (which included advice to Egypt, Syria, and Jordan that they recognize Israel and work for a peaceful solution to the Palestinian problem) often irritated other Arab leaders and led to endless bickering between Tunisia and the rest of the Arab world. Not that Bourguiba was wholly a man of peace amid warriors; in 1961 he ordered an attack on the French naval base at Bizerte (which the French had refused to abandon) that cost more than a thousand Tunisian lives—but the French left. At the same time he nationalized French property throughout Tunisia, yet he persuaded many French residents to remain in the country. A permanent friend of the Western powers, Bourguiba kept his nation solidly aligned with American policy— even going so far as to approve U.S. bombing raids on North Vietnam. He created a mixed economy—partly capitalist, partly nationalized—and presided over what he was fond of calling "Bourguibism," a kind of paternalistic road to Arab socialism. As he informed his fellow countrymen, "Abilities as great as Bourguiba's are not found around every corner. They are a miracle of nature that occurs rarely in history."

If when Tunisia achieved independence it inherited virtually intact the economic, industrial, and social structure developed under French occupation (for there was little large-scale fighting there), the same was not true of Algeria. The long, drawn-out, and terribly savage struggle for Algerian independence left that country a wasteland in 1962. More than a million of Algeria's nine million Moslems had been killed in the fighting; hundreds of thousands more had been uprooted by the French and forced into internment camps; many thousands more fled the country. Hundreds of villages had been destroyed, and severe damage had been done to such cities as Algiers and Oran. And since after 130 years of French rule few Moslems had been trained in any technical skills, when the *colons* fled in 1962 Algeria was left with virtually no doctors, engineers, or other specialists. In the coastal cities there were not even any firemen, for these too had been French.

But Algeria had abundant natural wealth on which to build, if this wealth could be organized efficiently. There were vast, rich farming areas and, of more immediate importance, large-scale oil and gas reserves in the interior. These, while not to be compared to the huge deposits of Saudi Arabia, would be sufficient to provide financing for reconstruction.

Algeria's first president was Ahmed Ben Bella, who for three years grappled with the nation's problems, mainly by forming large-scale cooperative farms to take over lands abandoned by the French and by introducing socialist measures to reorganize Algeria's shattered economy. At the same time he attempted to make Algiers the capital of the third world states of Africa. Claiming that in the face of Algeria's appalling domestic problems Ben Bella, despite his reforms, was devoting too much time and energy to foreign affairs, the Algerian army ousted him from office in June 1965. He was replaced by Colonel Houari Boumedienne, the former leader of the guerilla army that had placed Ben Bella in power.

In their years of power the French had purposely attempted to destroy the Algerian national identity—Algeria was, remember, to have been "united" with metropolitan France. Thus at the time of independence only 10 percent of Algeria's few teachers were Moslems; and very few Moslems were encouraged to go to school in the first place. So between the handful of educated revolutionary leaders and the vast mass of their followers there existed a tremendous cultural gap. This was aggravated by the fact that the great majority of Algerians were Berbers who (if they spoke anything but Berber) spoke French first, Arabic second. With problems such as these to face there could be no thought, for the present, of real democracy. Ben Bella, Boumedienne, and other Algerian leaders had little choice but to accept their role as a kind of ruling elite, sharing the economic privations of the rest of the nation while attempting to introduce their own special brand of Arab socialism from above. Like the early caliphs of Islam, their rule was austere, just, paternalistic—and very authoritarian.

Nationalization of the international oil company holdings in 1971 helped to strengthen Algeria's economy, and great progress was made in the field of mass education. Algeria devoted more than 11 percent of her national income to education—a tremendous proportion by any standards. Industrialization also proceeded, though at a slower pace. And in the end Ben Bella's dream was realized, for Algeria has become a major spokesman for the developing African third world nations.

Of all the North African states Morocco suffered least from French occupation, which was relatively brief and far more benign than elsewhere. After independence in 1956 the popular Sultan Mohammed V adopted the title of king with the intention of transforming his country into a constitutional monarchy. But Mohammed V died prematurely in February 1961, with most of his work not yet accomplished. His son, who now ascended the throne as Hassan II, lacked his father's energy, foresight, and political wisdom. Unable to maintain the rudimentary democratic forms he had inherited, Hassan dissolved parliament in 1965. Thereafter, though puppet parliaments came and went, the king ruled Morocco through his army.

But those who predicted an early end to Hassan's reign were mistaken. Using his prisons, his police, and his executioners as if he were a tenth-century sultan, Hassan survived two assassination attempts in 1972 and 1973; by playing off the ambitions of army leaders against the hopes of urban politicians, he kept his opponents disunited and at bay. It was a consummate

juggling act, strengthened in 1973 when he nationalized foreign business interests in Morocco, thus cur-
rying favor with the peasant masses. And when things
went wrong, he could always whip up enthusiastic support for his regime by loudly proclaiming his adherence
to the anti-Israeli *jihad*. The king's simple political
philosophy was summed up in his famous understate-
ment: "To say that power should belong to the nation
does not mean that everyone within this nation should
rule."

With this remark no doubt the sheikhs and princes
of the Arabian peninsula would be in total agreement.
For at the eastern end of the Arab world, as at the
western, archaic monarchies continued to rule. But the
story of this region in the years following the Second
World War may be perhaps best summed up in the
single word "oil." As we have seen, oil had been discovered in the independent Persian Gulf coast sheikhdoms even before the First World War; it was discovered in Saudi Arabia before the Second. Exploited first
by British petroleum companies and later (in Saudi
Arabia) by the huge Arabian-American Oil Company
(Aramco), oil brought increasing wealth to the desert
kingdoms. And with the dramatic increase both in
world consumption and in price that followed the end
of the Second World War, this wealth became a flood
of gold that transformed Arabia into a kind of twentieth-century Eldorado. As early as 1968 it was estimated that by 1988 Saudi Arabia's gold reserves would
equal those of the United States and Japan combined.

All of which was most welcome to the descendants
of Ibn Saud—welcome, but not absolutely vital. For to
King Faisal and the rest of the Saudi royal family,
what was vital was the preservation of Saudi society
on its rock-ribbed Islamic foundations. Once, when
asked whether all forms of socialism were equally dis-
tasteful to him, King Faisal replied, "We have the holy
Koran. . . . Why do we need socialism, capitalism, communism, or any other ideology?"

So during the 1960s Saudi Arabia emerged as a land of startling contrasts. It was a country of Rolls-Royce automobiles and camel caravans; a country that spent heavily on education but made sure that any male teachers of female students were blind; a country busily importing Western technology but banning alcoholic drinks, cinemas, and all but the most heavily censored television programs; a country in which women were encouraged to seek university degrees but forbidden to drive cars, work with men, or go unveiled in public. And the strict Islamic law was strictly enforced; thieves would have their hands chopped off by official swordsmen and adulteresses would be stoned to death (as a result, there is almost no theft in Saudi Arabia—as for adultery, statistics are lacking).

Because of their insistence on preserving their ancient culture at all costs Saudi Arabia's ruling family looked on Gamal Abdel Nasser's revolution in Egypt with suspicion and alarm. Arab socialism did not appeal to King Faisal any more than any other brand of socialism, and his fear of Soviet penetration of the Arab world was extreme. Yet, priding themselves on their guardianship of the holy cities of Mecca and Medina, the Saudis felt they must take a leading part in the struggle against Israel—to them, it really was a *jihad*. Their help to Egypt, Syria, and Jordan naturally took the form of financial subsidies. But since, in the case of Syria and Egypt at least, these subsidies were being employed to change Arab societies in socialist ways uncongenial to King Faisal, a very real conflict of interests developed. This division in Saudi aims was deepened by the fact that only through American support could the Saudis hope to maintain their uniquely Islamic society—yet the United States was Israel's chief ally.

Disliking Nasser and his social policies, King Faisal held Saudi Arabia aloof from Egyptian-Syrian strategy. He blamed both nations for encouraging Russian influence in Islam, and after the Six Day War disaster

he refused to finance the rebuilding of the Egyptian
and Syrian armies. Nasser's death in 1970 removed a
major obstacle to Saudi-Egyptian cooperation. King
Faisal even made a friendly visit to Cairo after Anwar
Sadat signed his treaty with the Soviet Union in 1971,
something that would have been unthinkable earlier.
But the shrewd Saudi monarch may have divined
Sadat's real intentions in the Near East—something
that the Egyptian president was at some pains to hide
from the rest of the world.

In some respects Anwar Sadat's position in the Arab
world was easier than Nasser's had been, precisely because he lacked Nasser's prestige. Less was expected
of him, and he was not the prisoner of any heroic nationalist poses. Furthermore, it seemed that the fierce
nationalistic pressure brought upon Egypt by her chief
ally, Syria, would be eased when, in November 1970,
a more moderate military regime seized power there
led by General Hafez Assad.

But of course Sadat remained the prisoner of Egyptian realities. The security of his government rested on
two things: the speed with which he could bring reform
and vitality to the Egyptian economy and the deci-
siveness with which he could redeem Egypt's military
humiliation. And both of these matters depended in
turn on the policy of the United States, the only power
in the world that could influence Israel. To meet American wishes in May 1971 Sadat announced his willingness to sign a formal peace treaty with (and therefore
recognize) Israel, as soon as Israeli forces were withdrawn from captured Arab territory. When this concession (which could have cost Sadat his presidency, and
which made him the target of Arab supranationalists
everywhere) brought no results, Sadat decided that the
military stalemate would have to be ended.

But to end it under Russian auspices would only
enrage the Americans and weld them closer to Israel.
So in July 1972, claiming that they were interfering
in Egypt's internal affairs, Sadat suddenly expelled all

Soviet technicians and military advisors from Egypt. This could only mean that Sadat was preparing for a reconciliation with the United States—but on what basis? His policy confused and angered Arabs everywhere, but especially in Cairo, where anti-Sadat riots took place in January 1973. Still the Egyptian president bided his time.

Then, suddenly, on Yom Kippur eve, October 6, 1973, Egyptian and Syrian forces struck against Israel. In rapid succession there followed the Russian shipment of arms to the Arab countries, the American airlift of weapons to Israel, the Israeli counterattack, the Soviet-American confrontation, the Arab oil embargo, and finally the UN-supervised cease-fire.

Although when the fighting ended on October 26 the Israelis had won again, Egyptian forces remained deep in Sinai. And above all, the results of the struggle represented a political triumph for the Arab world in general and for Anwar Sadat in particular. The Egyptians were justly proud of their part in the fighting (they suffered some sixty thousand casualties) and felt that the humiliations they had suffered at Israeli hands in the past were now redeemed in blood. This in turn meant that Sadat's hands were freed from the bonds of extreme nationalism. A victor to his own people, Anwar Sadat could now lead them where he chose— and, even before the Yom Kippur War, he had selected a daring departure from tradition on the road ahead.

Jerusalem—and Beyond

Of Anwar Sadat's two primary aims in launching the Yom Kippur War, one had been the easing of nationalist tensions at home by applying the balm of a victory; the other had been to blast the United States from its stand-pat position regarding the Near East. He was successful in achieving both objectives.

The reappraisal of American policy toward the Arab world by the Nixon administration and its chief diplomatic strategist, Dr. Henry Kissinger, was swift. Their Israeli ally had come perilously close to disaster; the world itself had come to the brink of Armageddon, and although the United States might survive without Arab oil for a while, it could not do so indefinitely. All of which might have been foreseen had American leaders paid any attention to recent Near Eastern developments. But, intent on establishing relations with China and broadening détente with the Soviet Union,

American officials had neglected their homework in this area.

For it was inevitable that sooner or later an Israeli nation of some one and a half million would be hard pressed to defend itself against neighboring enemies whose populations exceeded fifty million; it was inevitable that sooner or later the two blustering superpowers, if they maintained their irresponsible rivalry in the Near East, would be brought into direct confrontation; and it was inevitable that sooner or later the oil problem would arise to haunt the West in one form or another. Inevitable because under current rates of consumption Near Eastern oil reserves would run dry within a foreseeable future. Even before October 1973 Arab leaders had been warning that they would have to cut back production. Inevitable also had been the fivefold increase in oil prices imposed by OPEC after 1973—for oil had long been one of the cheapest commodities in the world, badly underpriced, as were all raw materials extracted from the former European colonial empires. When the Arabs raised oil prices they were simply shaking off the last chains of foreign exploitation—and if this brought economic crisis to the industrial societies of the West, then it must be remembered that the prosperity of those societies had for nearly two centuries rested upon their ruthless exploitation of underdeveloped nations.

So Dr. Kissinger boarded his magic carpet and flew back and forth from Washington to various Near Eastern capitals and between those capitals and Jerusalem. He promised Sadat and other Arab leaders that henceforth American policy in the Near East would be more "even-handed" and warned Israelis that they must now make concessions to gain peace. Suddenly the United States emerged as a friend to the Arab world; American money and technology now began to flow to Egypt, Saudi Arabia, and any other Arab nation that would accept its aid.

Perhaps the most glaring symbol of the new American-Arab relationship was President Richard Nixon's visit to Cairo and other Arab capitals in June 1974. There he was enthusiastically greeted by throngs who neither knew nor cared about his domestic difficulties but rather saw in him the prophet of a new era.

But not all Arabs were pleased. The Syrians (still depending on Soviet weapons) were suspicious that Nixon and Kissinger intended only to split the Arab world. Palestinians were certain that improved Arab-American relations would be constructed only upon the ruins of their hopes. Some of the Palestinian leaders, including PLO chairman and al-Fatah chief Yasir Arafat, decided that perhaps they ought now to abandon their aim of wiping Israel from the map and settle for the creation of a Palestinian state on the West Bank, which had been seized by Israel in 1967. This policy was bitterly opposed by the more radical Palestinians, but Arafat carried a majority of his followers with him. His more moderate policy brought some rewards: European statesmen began admitting that the Palestinians were indeed a people deserving of a homeland of their own; and on November 13, 1974, Yasir Arafat, wearing his guerrilla fighter's costume and with a pistol at his belt, addressed the United Nations General Assembly. "I have come bearing an olive branch," he said, "and a freedom fighter's gun. Do not let the olive branch fall from my hand."

But while Palestinian terrorist attacks against Israel continued, Anwar Sadat made that new departure in Arab policy for which the Yom Kippur War had opened the way. On September 1, 1975, under American auspices, Egypt and Israel signed a so-called interim agreement that amounted to a total armistice. By its terms the Israelis agreed to withdraw their forces from certain advanced positions in the Sinai desert in return for an Egyptian promise not to attack. To ensure compliance American civilian observers were stationed at observance posts between the two armies—hostages to peace.

The various Palestinian liberation organizations and Arab nationalists from Casablanca to Baghdad angrily denounced this Israeli-Egyptian détente and accused Sadat of betraying Islam. Their fury was in inverse proportion to their impotence, for without Egypt there could be no hope for any future military assault against Israel. But the Egyptian people, who for thirty years had suffered the lion's share of casualties in this *jihad*, enthusiastically supported their president. So too (privately) did the Saudi Arabians, whose oil riches continued to finance much of Egypt's tottering economy. Jordan's King Hussein—chastised by defeat in 1967, civil war against the Palestinians in 1970, and now increasingly dependent on American financial aid—expressed cautiously polite disapproval. Of the "front line" Arab states, only Syria remained violently opposed to Sadat's policies. But the Syrians were soon to find themselves fully occupied elsewhere.

Elsewhere was Lebanon, which ever since the days of the French mandate had maintained a precarious stability between its Moslem and Christian inhabitants through a unique constitution that evenly divided political power between the two groups. But with the influx of Palestinian refugees following Israeli independence in 1948 that balance had begun to wobble; when even more Palestinians fled to Lebanon from Jordan following Black September, the balance was destroyed. The Palestinians demanded (as they had in Jordan) that they be allowed to carry out terrorist raids against the Israelis from their camps in Lebanon. The Lebanese government, which had maintained circumspect neutrality throughout the anti-Israeli *jihad*, refused, but lacked the military power to really restrain the Palestinians or to protect themselves against the inevitable Israeli reprisals. Under these pressures Lebanon simply collapsed during 1976 into an increasingly violent and bloody civil war. Lebanese conser-

The Arab World Today

vative Christians, supported occasionally by Israeli forces, battled Lebanese Moslems led by radical Palestinians in a conflict that utterly destroyed what had been a relatively liberal, enlightened, pluralistic, and prosperous society.

The Syrians, fearing that chaos in Lebanon might invite Israeli intervention (as indeed it did in the south, where Israeli forces occupied a twenty-mile-deep "security zone" in the troubled country), sent large, regular army forces into Lebanon in June 1977, to restore order, disarm the combatants, and enforce a general cease-fire. They were followed by a United Nations force, which took up positions along the Israeli-Lebanese border in the south. The Israelis thereupon withdrew from their "security zone," but the Syrians remained—to become ever more embroiled in the bloody complexities of a nation that had dissolved into rival nationalisms, private armies, and gang warfare. An uneasy peace, punctuated by savage gun battles in ravaged Beirut, was thus temporarily maintained in this sensitive area.

Perhaps impelled by the dangerous situation in Lebanon, Anwar Sadat now took another and even more daring step along the road to Near Eastern peace. In October 1977 he informed American journalists that if invited he would be pleased to go personally to Israel in order to confer face-to-face with Israeli Prime Minister Menachem Begin. The Israelis immediately responded to this hint; and on November 19, 1977, the unthinkable occurred: Anwar Sadat, president of Egypt and the most powerful leader in the Arab world, entered Jerusalem as the guest of the Israeli government, there to address the Israeli Knesset (parliament) on the subject of real and lasting peace. It was as great a miracle as any that had ever taken place in that city of miracles. But Sadat was only acting in the spirit of an older, greater, and more liberal tradition of Arab statesmanship. For more than a century that tradition had been submerged in the blood and rhetoric of nationalism and the Arab struggle for independence—but as Sadat demonstrated, it remained vitally inherent in the culture of Islam.

His very presence before them, Sadat told the Knesset, demonstrated that Arabs and Jews could and would be friends. The existence of the state of Israel would now be recognized as a permanent and peacefully acceptable fact of life; the *jihad* was ended. In return for this Sadat asked that Israel relinquish all Arab territory conquered during the Six Day War of 1967 and permit the establishment of an independent Palestinian state in Gaza and along the West Bank of the River Jordan.

While enthusiastically welcoming the Egyptian president's gesture of friendship, the Israelis found some of his conditions unacceptable. Having fought for thirty years to maintain a precarious toehold in their ancient homeland, Israelis were understandably worried about their future security. While they were perfectly willing to restore all of Sinai to Egyptian sovereignty, they were not prepared to withdraw their occupation forces from the volatile West Bank—an area Prime Minister Begin ominously (to Arab ears) described by its ancient Hebraic names, Judea and Samaria. The establishment there of an independent Palestinian state, inevitably to be dominated by Yasir Arafat's PLO terrorist organization, was something no Israeli government could lightly contemplate. As for the old Arab quarter of Jerusalem—in the days of Solomon and David this had been an integral part of the capital of Israel, and having been won back during the Six Day War, it would never again be relinquished. And finally, though Sadat might speak with authority for Egypt, how could he possibly guarantee the adherence of Jordan, Syria, and the Palestinians to any permanent settlement?

This last question was immediately underscored when Syria, Jordan, Libya, Algeria, Morocco, Iraq, and the Palestinian liberation organizations convened an anti-Israel, anti-Sadat, antipeace meeting in Damascus as soon as the Egyptian president returned to Cairo. But aside from agreeing on what they were against, the so-called rejectionist leaders could not seem to agree on what they favored; and the political initiative remained with Anwar Sadat.

Of course both Sadat and Begin could easily and quickly have concluded peace between Egypt and Israel, for neither side had any territorial or important economic demands to make on the other; Israel had only to return the conquered parts of the Sinai to Egypt. But both men were in a very real sense constrained by their personal and political heritages. Sadat did not feel he could simply abdicate responsibility for Arab interests beyond Egypt, especially the interests of the powerless Palestinian people. Begin on the other hand felt not only a responsibility to the somber shades of Jewish history but also to the security of future generations of Israelis in a hostile environment. It was not surprising then that negotiations between Egypt and Israel dragged on fruitlessly throughout the next nine months and finally, during the summer of 1978, stalled completely.

In a dramatic attempt to salvage something from Sadat's peace initiative of the previous November, American President Jimmy Carter announced in mid-August 1978 that Sadat and Prime Minister Begin would meet with him at the presidential retreat in Camp David, Maryland. Disaster was confidently predicted for this final effort to prevent yet another Near Eastern war; but Carter, Sadat, and Begin confounded the pessimists. During a grueling conference that lasted from September 5 to September 17 the three leaders hammered out two separate accords—one regarding a peace treaty to be concluded within three months between Egypt and Israel, the other a Five Year Plan for settlement of the West Bank and Palestinian issues. Rejoicing was great in Cairo, Jerusalem, and Washington—but premature. For haggling over the fine points of the Camp David accords was to continue yet another six months until finally, on March 10, 1979, President Carter, gambling all the prestige of his office, flew personally to Cairo and then Jerusalem in one last, bold bid for peace. During the President's five-day pilgrimage American pressure upon both Egyptians and Israelis was prompted by a new and dire sense of urgency.

That urgency was ignited by explosive events in nearby Iran. There, at the call of their revered religious leader, the Ayatollah Khomeini, the Iranian people rose in revolution against their King of Kings, Shah Mohammed Reza Pahlevi. During the first two months of 1979, after bloody rioting throughout the country, the Shah, his generals, his hated secret police (the dreaded SAVAK), and the entire ancient apparatus of royal tyranny were overthrown. But this was not simply a Western-style uprising of suffering masses against an oppressive government. The Iranian rebellion was, in large part, an *Islamic* upheaval—an attempt by fervently religious Moslem masses to "cleanse" their society not only of royal dictatorship, but also of the "irreligious" and "decadent" modern social institutions which that dictatorship had "forced" upon the nation.

With their insistence that Iran become an "Islamic Republic," ruled according to the precepts of the Koran and governed by Ayatollahs, Imams, and other religious leaders, the Iranian rebels reminded some Western observers of the puritanical Almoravides and Almohades of ancient North Africa and Spain. Although Iran was not an Arab nation and its people were overwhelmingly of the Shia sect rather than the Sunni majority, fears were nevertheless aroused of a rebirth of religious fanaticism throughout Islam.

These fears were, most probably, groundless. Nations struggling toward industrialization, social democracy, and a better economic life for their peoples cannot long be governed successfully according to ar-

chaic religious texts. Just a few days after the Shah
fled his former domains, thousands of Iranian women
were demonstrating *against* the Ayatollah Khomeini's
command that they once again retire from universities,
industry, and public life to the seclusion of their
veils and homes. The clock could not be turned
back in Iran—and certainly not in neighboring Arab
states.

Nonetheless, under the threat of new religious and
political upheavals, Sadat and Begin hastened to accept President Carter's new compromise proposals.
Peace treaties between Egypt and Israel were finally
signed, sealed, and ratified on March 30, 1979. A few
days later as the guest of Anwar Sadat, Israeli Prime
Minister Menachem Begin at long last visited the pyramids outside Cairo—those mighty monuments Begin
always mistakenly insisted had been raised by the
slave labor of his earliest ancestors. Sadat himself was
cheered by millions of his fellow Egyptians as the man
of peace—a title he well deserved. Not since the days
of Sulaiman the Magnificent had any Islamic leader
made such an impact upon world affairs.

The dawn of peace between Egypt and Israel was
not a cloudless sky, however. The endlessly vexing
problems regarding the future status of the West Bank
and Jerusalem, of the future of the Palestinian exiles,
remained to be solved. And of course the "rejectionist"
leaders of other Arab states and the PLO thundered
against Sadat's "betrayal" of their Holy War. But despite an increase in al-Fatah's terrorist activities
against Israel and Yasir Arafat's thinly disguised
threats to assassinate Sadat, it seemed that peace in
the Near East might have achieved a head start on its
enemies which they would be hard put to overcome.

And as the fires of Arab nationalism began to flicker
out, it appeared that older Arab traditions of tolerance
and pluralism might once again begin to flourish—as
might the native Arab political genius for unity in di-
versity and personal freedom in religious faith. There

was great need for these qualities—not only in the realms of Islam, but throughout a fearful world and among people of all faiths, *in the Name of God, the Compassionate, the Merciful....*

Abu-Lughod, Ibrahim A. *The Arab Rediscovery of Europe.* Princeton, N.J.: Princeton University Press, 1963.

Addison James T. *The Christian Approach to the Moslem.* New York: Columbia University Press, 1942.

Ali, Ameer. *A Short History of the Saracens.* London: Macmillan, 1924.

American-Christian Palestine Committee. *The Arab War Effort.* New York: ACPC, 1946.

Antonius, George. *The Arab Awakening.* Philadelphia: Lippincott, 1939.

Arnold, Sir Thomas W. *The Caliphate.* Oxford: Clarendon Press, 1924.

————, and Guillaume, A., eds. *The Legacy of Islam.* Oxford: Clarendon Press, 1931.

Awad, Mahmoud M. *A Challenge to the Arabs.* New York: Pageant Press, 1954.

Azzam, Abdel Rahman. *Eternal Message of Muhammad,* trans. C. E. Farah. New York: Devin-Adair, 1964.

Berque, Jacques. *The Arabs: Their History and Future,* trans. J. Stewart. New York: Praeger, 1964.

Blyden, Edward W. *Christianity, Islam and the Negro Race.* Edinburgh: Edinburgh University Press, 1967.

Browne, Lawrence E. *The Prospects of Islam.* London: S.C.M. Press, 1944.

Burton, Sir Richard F. *The Jew, The Gypsy and El Islam.* London: Hutchinson, 1898.

Bury, George W. *Pan-Islam.* London: Macmillan, 1919.

Byford-Jones, W. *Forbidden Frontiers.* London: Hale, 1958.

Byng, Edward J. *The World of the Arabs.* Boston: Little, Brown, 1944.

Carmichael, Joel. *The Shaping of the Arab.* New York: Macmillan, 1967.

Childers, Erskine B. *Common Sense about the Arab World.* New York: Macmillan, 1960.

Coupland, Sir Reginald. *East Africa and Its Invaders.* Oxford: Clarendon Press, 1938.

Cragg, Kenneth. *The Call of the Minaret.* New York: Oxford University Press, 1956.

Cremeans, Charles D. *The Arabs and the World.* New York: Praeger, 1963.

Davis, William S. *A Short History of the Near East.* New York: Macmillan, 1937.

Dermenghem, Emile. *Muhammad and the Islamic Tradition,* trans. J. Watt. New York: Harper and Bros., 1958.

Dib, Georges M. *The Arab Bloc in the United Nations.* Amsterdam: Djambatan, 1956.

Douglas-Home, Charles. *The Arabs and Israel.* Chester Springs, Pa: Dufour, 1968.

Eliot, Sir Charles N. E. *Turkey in Europe.* London: Arnold, 1908.

Freeman, Edward E. *History and Conquests of the Saracens.* London: Macmillan, 1876.

Gabriel, Francesco. *The Arab Revival.* New York: Random House, 1961.

Gibb, H. A. R. *Modern Trends in Islam.* Chicago: University of Chicago Press, 1947.

———, ed. *Encyclopaedia of Islam.* Leiden: E. J. Brill, 1960.

Gilman, Arthur. *The Saracens.* New York: Putnam and Sons, 1908.

Glubb, Sir John Bagot. *The Course of Empire.* Englewood Cliffs, N.J.: Prentice-Hall, 1965.

———. *The Empire of the Arabs.* Englewood Cliffs, N.J.: Prentice-Hall, 1963.

———. *The Great Arab Conquests.* Englewood Cliffs, N.J.: Prentice-Hall, 1964.

Grant, Christina P. *The Syrian Desert.* New York: Macmillan, 1938.

Graves, Robert. *Lawrence and the Arabs.* London: Cape, 1927.

Hasan, Yusuf. *The Arabs and the Sudan.* Edinburgh: Edinburgh University Press, 1967.

Hitti, Phillip K. *A History of the Arabs*. New York: St. Martin's Press, 1956.

Hodgkin, E. C. *The Arabs*. London: Oxford University Press, 1966.

Hosali, Nina. *North African Diary*. London: SPANA, 1947.

Hourami, Albert H. *Arabic Thought in the Liberal Age*. New York: Oxford University Press, 1962.

Irving, Washington. *Mahomet and His Successors*. New York: Putnam and Sons, 1868.

Izzedin, Nejla M. *The Arab World*. Chicago: Regnery, 1953.

Jarvic, C. *Yesterday and Today in Sinai*. Boston: Houghton, Mifflin, 1932.

Jeffrey, Arthur, ed. *A Reader on Islam*. 's-Gravenhage: Mouton, 1962.

Kadduri, Majid. *War and Peace in the Law of Islam*. Baltimore: Johns Hopkins, 1955.

Katiba, Habeeb I. *The New Spirit in Arab Lands*. New York: Author, 1940.

Kimche, Jon. *Seven Fallen Pillars*. New York: Praeger, 1953.

Lamb, Harold. *The Crusades*. Garden City, N.Y.: Doubleday-Doran, 1931.

Landau, Rom. *Islam and the Arabs*. New York: Macmillan, 1959.

Lawrence, Thomas E. *The Seven Pillars of Wisdom*. Garden City, N.Y.: Doran and Co., 1935.

Lewis, Bernard. *The Arabs in History*. New York: Harper, 1960.

Lane-Poole, Stanley. *The Mohammedan Dynasties*. Westminister: Constable, 1894.

Mahmud, Sayyid Fayyaz. *A Short History of Islam*. Karachi: Oxford University Press, 1960.

Mansfield, Peter. *The Arab World*. New York: Crowell, 1976.

Muir, Sir William. *The Caliphate*. Edinburgh: Grant, 1915.

Myers, Eugene A. *Arabic Thought and the Western World in the Golden Age of Islam*. New York: Ungar, 1964.

Nuseibeh, Hazem Zaki. *The Ideas of Arab Nationalism*. Ithaca: Cornell University Press, 1956.

Nutting, Anthony. *The Arabs*. New York: Potter, 1964.

O'Leary, De Lacy E. *Arabic Thought and Its Place in History.* New York: E. P. Dutton, 1922.

Partner, Peter. *A Short Political Guide to the Arab World.* New York: Praeger, 1960.

Payne, Pierre S. R. *The Holy Sword.* New York: Harper, 1959.

Rodwell, J. M., trans. *The Koran.* New York: E. P. Dutton, 1974.

Roosevelt, Kermit. *Arabs, Oil and History.* New York: Harper, 1949.

Rosa, Guido. *North Africa Speaks.* New York: John Day, 1946.

Saab, Hassan. *The Arab Federalists of the Ottoman Empire.* Amsterdam: Djambatan, 1958.

Sayegh, Fayez Abdullah. *Arab Unity.* New York: Devin-Adair, 1958.

Scott, Samuel P. *History of the Moorish Empire in Europe.* Philadelphia: Lippincott, 1904.

Smith, Henry. *The Bible and Islam.* New York: Scribner's, 1897.

Smith, William C. *Islam and Modern History.* Princeton, N.J.: Princeton University Press, 1957.

Spector, Ivan. *The Soviet Union and the Muslim World.* Seattle: Washington University Press, 1959.

Spuler, Bertold. *The Muslim World.* Leiden: E. J. Brill, 1960.

Thomas, Bertram. *The Arabs.* London: Butterworth, 1937.

Van Ess, John. *Meet the Arab.* New York: John Day, 1943.

Villiers, Allan J. *Sons of Sinbad.* New York: Scribner's, 1969.

Von Grunebaum, Gustave E. *Medieval Islam.* Chicago: University of Chicago Press, 1953.

Wakehurst, John de Vere. *The Truth about Mesopotamia, Palestine and Syria.* London: Allen and Unwin, 1923.

Wismar, Adolph. *A Study in Tolerance.* New York: Columbia University Press, 1927.

SUGGESTED READING

The Empire of the Arabs, The Great Arab Conquests, and *The Course of Empire,* all by Sir John Bagot Glubb, former British commander of the Jordanian Arab Legion, make a marvelously detailed, thoughtful, and colorful narrative from the birth of the Prophet to about A.D. 1500.

Phillip Hitti's *A History of the Arabs* is magisterial and carries the story up to the early 1950s.

Washington Irving's *Mahomet and His Successors* is history in the grand tradition of the old school—that is to say, eminently readable.

The Arab World by Peter Mansfield is valuable for its résumé of events since 1950.

T. E. Lawrence's great work *The Seven Pillars of Wisdom* is perhaps the finest single book ever to have been written about Islam. But it is very long. Impatient readers are referred to his *War in the Desert,* a shorter, earlier version of *The Seven Pillars of Wisdom.* Concerning the legendary Lawrence of Arabia, there is also Robert Graves's excellent study, *Lawrence and the Arabs.*

For a brief, comprehensive, penetrating overview of Arab history, Bernard Lewis's *The Arabs in History* remains unchallenged.

Index